740009834412

GIANT GEORGE

In 2006, Dave and Christie Nasser bought a Great Dane puppy. They named him George and from a quivering misfit he grew into a gentle giant. In 2010, George was crowned by the Guinness Book of World Records as the Tallest Dog in the World, ever. He's appeared on Oprah and has his own global fan club. At five feet tall and seven feet long he is still a big softie, eager to play and boisterous to the point of causing chaos. *Giant George* is the heart-warming story of a much-cherished pet, who continues to make Dave and Christie happy.

Books by Lynne Barrett-Lee
Published by The House of Ulverscroft:

ONE DAY, SOMEDAY

DAVE NASSER
WITH LYNNE BARRETT-LEE

◆

GIANT GEORGE
LIFE WITH THE BIGGEST
DOG IN THE WORLD

Complete and Unabridged

ULVERSCROFT
Leicester

First published in Great Britain in 2011 by
Simon & Schuster UK Ltd., London

First Large Print Edition
published 2012
by arrangement with
Simon & Schuster UK Ltd.
A CBS Company, London

British Library CIP Data

Nasser, Dave, *1966* –
Giant George.
1. Nasser, Dave, *1966* – 2. Nasser, Christie.
3. George (Dog) 4. Great Dane- -Anecdotes.
5. Dog owners- -Arizona- -Tucson- -Anecdotes.
6. Large type books.
I. Title II. Barrett-Lee, Lynne, *1959* –
636.7′3–dc23

ISBN 978–1–4448–1138–4

Published by
F. A. Thorpe (Publishing)
Anstey, Leicestershire

Set by Words & Graphics Ltd.
Anstey, Leicestershire
Printed and bound in Great Britain by
T. J. International Ltd., Padstow, Cornwall

This book is printed on acid-free paper

Contents

1

Life's Mistakes

Arizona Daily Star
Offered: Pets
HOME NEEDED FOR
GREAT DANE PUPPY
Four-month-old blue Great Dane
puppy needs a home now.
Call Dave on 1 521 1976.

Sometimes in life you make mistakes. It was the end of March 2006 in Tucson, Arizona — a particularly beautiful time of year — and open in front of me was a copy of the *Arizona Daily Star*. It was carrying the ad I'd placed there a week back, for the ridiculous sum of $40.

I did a quick calculation in my head. I'd already laid out $1,750 for our puppy, plus the cost of around six weeks' worth of specialist puppy food, an extra large crate, a leash and a collar, dog bowls — both food and water — and now this ad. We were a cool

1

$2,000 out of pocket by now, I reckoned, but I didn't care. I was out of patience. I was seriously stressed. I was at the end of my rope.

The ad had already attracted about a dozen phone calls, and two of them seemed to be genuine possibilities. One was from a woman who worked at the local animal organisation in Tucson. When I explained to her that George had become a lot more than I could handle, she reacted excitedly. It was obvious right away that she was a serious dog lover, and she wanted our puppy pretty badly. The other call was from a guy who lived a couple of hours away, up in Phoenix. He said he already had a couple of Great Danes in the family, and would very much love to have a third.

So, job done. With my wife's very reluctant agreement, I had one decision left to make: who should have him? Whose home should he go to? George, who was never far from Christie and me — ever — was sitting on the floor beside my chair while I was thinking about this, as if he knew that, right now, it was the best place for him to be. I glanced down, and saw the sparkle in his intensely blue eyes. It was the same sparkle that had first attracted us to him, the same sparkle that had Christie fall in love with him on sight.

Did he know? Was he already preparing for the worst? Was he already resigned to being put in yet another crate and shipped off some place else?

But George didn't seem to be thinking about himself. While I mused about how much had already happened in his short life, he seemed more concerned about me. He lifted himself up, tipped his head to one side and looked at me with an expression that I'd already come to know. 'Hey, Dad,' it seemed to say to me. 'What's up?'

He then did something that would be appropriate if you were writing a scene for a movie. He got up from the floor and put his head in my lap, then looked up at me with those enormous blue eyes.

I looked back at the ad, to the two numbers I'd scribbled down, and I realised that, actually, I couldn't let him go. He was part of our family, and no matter what the hassle, no matter what the pain, one thing you don't give up on is family. It was time to step up and be the bigger man.

I balled the ad in my fist, and launched it inexpertly towards the bin. It missed, but what the hell. It was time to make the calls. Sometimes in life you make mistakes.

★   ★   ★

And often in life you make compromises too, because relationships are all about compromise. My compromise, made one day in the summer of 2005, had been a pretty sensible one, I thought. I wanted to move back to Tucson, Arizona — my home town — and it was clear that my then wife-to-be was less keen. We had already agreed — sort of — to move there soon, and she was busy looking for a job, so it wasn't a case of 'wouldn't', more a case of 'would, grudgingly'. I wanted the move to be special for both of us, hence the conversation. It turned out that she could be bribed.

'A dog?' I asked, seeing her determined expression and realising this was probably a non-negotiable part of the deal.

Christie nodded. 'Yes. When we move to Arizona, I want a dog. After all, we'll have a house. We'll have a yard. We'll have the space . . . '

This left me pretty much out of excuses.

★　★　★

Christie had always been a dog lover. I, on the other hand, wasn't, though we did have dogs in the family. Growing up, my brother and I had two toy poodles. They were called Apollo and Sugar, and both of them had plenty of character. Had Apollo, in particular, been entered in an *America's Funniest Home Videos* contest, he probably could have won it. He would get up on two front legs, then walk along and pee at the same time — not a skill with an awful lot of practical application, but one that would have everyone in stitches.

Even so, though Apollo and Sugar were very much part of the family, I'd never considered myself a 'dog lover' particularly. Both of them died when I was in my teens, and I had no desire, once I'd grown up and moved to California, to get another, even had I lived somewhere suitable. As a consequence, I'd spent my adult life in a dog-free — indeed, pet-free — environment. And that was just how I liked it. Dogs meant responsibility, commitment, hassle: all things I was happy to live without.

Christie, who'd been raised in Seal Beach, in Orange County, California — a beautiful place right on the coast — had a dog when she was growing up, too. The dog was a Dalmatian-Cockapoo cross called Spot, who'd been in the family since before Christie was born. Theirs was a pleasant enough, but not really loving relationship. Perhaps because she felt she'd been usurped by Christie coming along, maybe because she'd always hated the name Spot or possibly because she was just a pretty grouchy sort of dog, Spot didn't seem to like her a whole lot, Christie told me. They got along, but they certainly didn't bond.

Spot died when Christie was about fourteen years old and she'd always planned, once she had a home of her own, to have a dog of her own too — one who was *her* dog, and loved her right back. So meeting me wouldn't have been the most productive move ever, in that regard, had I not seen the writing on the wall. My fiancée wanted a dog and I wanted to make my fiancée happy: if it made her happy to have a dog join the family, then so be it.

'Okay, then,' I said, feeling this might be the clincher. 'We move to Tucson, and we get ourselves a dog.'

★   ★   ★

When I met Christie, in the fall of 2003, I wasn't really looking to settle down. I was free of commitments, and enjoying that freedom, so the state of affairs suited me fine. I was thirty-eight years old, and despite my parents' endless comments about how the situation needed to change, I wasn't in any rush to get married. I'd left Tucson for Los Angeles in order to go to college and study economics, having been seduced by California and everything it had to offer. I'd seen no reason since then to return to Arizona. Sure, Arizona was okay, and Tucson was too, but I had a good life, and a good business — pretty much everything I needed, in fact. What needed to change?

In one respect, however, I wasn't perhaps as happy as I made out. I'd recently come out of a long-term relationship when I met Christie and though I was over it and getting on with life, I was probably still a bit vulnerable deep down. And, I guess, I was keen to play things cool. We were originally set up by my sister-in-law, who had sensibly figured out that since the person I ended up with would be related to her, it made sense to have a hand in the choosing. Also, Christie was her friend, so she knew both of us pretty well, and she felt sure we would get along.

And she'd been right. Christie was really attractive and fiercely independent — something I realised straight away. On our first date, we went out to a sports bar in Long Beach, and had drinks and some food. We had a relaxed, enjoyable time, but when it came time to pay the bill, Christie toughened up. There was no way she was going to let me pay her half. I liked that. Not because I didn't want to pay — I tried my best — but because

I recognised that here was someone who wanted things on her terms. She was her own woman, and that's how she's stayed.

She was also great company; she was intelligent and feisty, and we started going out all the time. Despite my initial determination not to get too involved (some might say this had become my modus operandi), I realised that Christie and I had something good going on. Pretty soon we were serious and it was becoming ever more obvious that life without her no longer seemed so attractive.

It took less than a year for me to reach the decision that this was the girl I was going to marry. Marry, that was, if she'd have me, and I wasn't completely sure she would yet. I planned my proposal carefully. It was December and we'd arranged to go to brunch. I'd booked a lovely outdoor restaurant that was sited on a clifftop; the balcony overlooked a large expanse of water, and the whole setting was pretty romantic. It was classy, too — the kind of place that gives you a bowl of mixed berries to nibble on while you sip your drinks and decide what to order. Christie had no idea what I'd planned to do over brunch, and the ring was burning a hole in my pocket; I couldn't remember the last time I'd been so nervous, and I knew I'd have no appetite till I'd popped the question. I was getting more antsy by the second. Hell, this was something I had never done in my entire life, and I couldn't stop rehearsing the words in my head. Will you marry me? . . . Would you like to marry me? . . . Would you consider being my wife? . . . I just couldn't seem to settle on the right words. It was almost like a job interview — really stressful.

As it turned out, there was a short wait while they made our table ready, so they sat us in this area with a fabulous view. It was private, too, with only one other couple waiting near us, and they'd been seated quite a way away.

'Your menu, madam?' said a waiter, handing her this big leather-bound tome. 'And yours, sir?' he added, giving me mine.

Decided, I put mine on my lap. My hands were getting sweaty, I noticed. Crazy . . . Christie had already opened her menu and started looking at it. Then she stopped, and peered over the top of it at me.

'You okay, Dave?' she asked. 'You seem really uptight today.'

'That's because I am,' I said, pretty much bursting with the weight of it. How'd this happen? I was a man nearly in my forties, for goodness sake. She frowned then, too, and put down her menu as well.

'So,' she said, looking a bit concerned now. 'What's up?'

'Erm,' I said, rummaging in my pocket for the ring box.

Christie blinked at me, waiting, then said, 'Well?'

The waiter was approaching, so I guessed our table must be ready. My timing, it seemed, was pretty lousy.

'Erm,' I said again (or, to be accurate, 'erm' was what came out). 'Christie, would you like to be my wife?'

'Oh!' she said, blinking some more. 'Oh, now I get it! For a minute there, you were starting to have me worried.'

'So is that a yes?' I said, finally wrestling the box from my jacket.

'Your table's ready now, sir,' said the waiter.

She kept me waiting, of course — right until we were seated at the table, when she finally put me out of my misery by leaning across and mouthing the word 'yes'. The ring was the right size, and lunch was pretty good too.

We were married in September 2005.

* * *

Getting away from LA and back to my home town seemed a natural extension to our starting our new life together. And, for Christie at least, getting a dog was part of this. So while I searched for the perfect house for us, she searched for a perfect pet. She'd started poring over the small ads in the papers even before we'd begun packing up.

She had her heart set on getting something big. There were numerous breeds on her shortlist initially, including Rhodesian Ridgebacks and Labrador Retrievers, but there was something about Great Danes and Weimaraners we both liked, so the choice narrowed down pretty quickly. She'd done plenty of research on the Internet, too, and eventually we settled on a Dane. Apparently, if it was a large breed you were after, a Great Dane was the best dog to go for. They fit the bill perfectly as family pets, being quiet, shambling dogs who didn't bark a lot and weren't prone to tearing a house apart. They also, and I was particularly pleased to hear this, didn't have a tendency to chew up your prized possessions or shed hair all over the furniture. But, like many breeds of pedigree dog, they were also pretty hard to track down. Even with the amount of time she'd committed to doing so, by the time we'd moved to Tucson, Christie still hadn't found a puppy.

I wasn't too fussed about this myself. We'd moved into an apartment while we were searching for a house — a small two bed, two bath place, where I could set up the second bedroom as an office. It was pretty, with half the rooms looking out over a small courtyard, but it was also a bit cramped, and it seemed sensible to me to wait until we'd found a house to get our puppy. Quite apart from the unsuitability of keeping a dog in an apartment, there was also the small matter of the terms of our lease — we were not *allowed* to keep a dog in our apartment.

Christie, however, had other ideas, and dismissed my natural concerns about this little detail. She wanted to get her pet now — right away — perhaps because it was just in her nature to be impetuous, or perhaps because she worried that if she left it too long I might mount a rearguard action and change my mind. But there weren't any Great Dane puppies in Tucson, nor in Phoenix. In fact, it didn't look like there were any in the whole state of Arizona.

One of the reasons for the shortage was timing: you had to find puppies that were old enough to leave their mothers, and this was clearly not a peak time of year. The other was a product of the pedigree dog business. Many breeders were pretty reluctant — quite rightly, I guess — to let their puppies go without attaching a set of conditions about the people they went to and their background, and what was going to happen next. Because of this, some already had long waiting lists for pups, some required references about your previous dog history, and some insisted on things such as committing to the show circuit and training your puppy in a very specific way — to walk on your left at all times, as they did in show rings, for example. Some would expect you to commit either to allowing your dog to breed and/or to letting the breeder have first pick of any next generation pups. It was as though they retained control of them. But we didn't want these sorts of strings attached to *our* pup — all we wanted was a family pet.

Eventually our sights drifted further afield — back to California, and to an ad Christie spotted that had been placed online in the *LA Times*. It was early January by now, and it had been placed by a breeder based in Oregon.

'Phone them,' instructed Christie, when she left for work that morning. 'I have a good feeling about this one. And we must be quick, or else we'll miss the boat again.'

As we still didn't have even a sniff of a suitable house, I wasn't worried about missing any boats, of course. But I also knew better than *not* to ring the woman, not when Christie had that telltale gleam in her eye.

'The parents are real big,' the woman told me, once I'd got through and told her I was interested. 'The mom is one hundred and sixty pounds, and the dad is two hundred.'

And in an incredible feat of not really listening to what she was telling me (Why did that even matter? Great Danes were big dogs, weren't they?), I took this in and then completely forgot about it, as I was more interested in jotting down all the other stuff she was telling me about which of the pups were still available for sale.

'Tell you what,' she said, 'why don't I email you a picture of them all, then you and your wife can decide which one might suit you?'

Christie was understandably excited when she came home from work, particularly when she learned that the puppies were ready to leave their mother (they'd been born on 17 November), and even more so when she looked at the picture. It was a real sight — a chaotic jumble of paws and snouts and tails. There were thirteen in the litter altogether. Twelve of these were entangled with one another, as young puppies tend to be, but our eyes were immediately drawn to one pup who was standing apart from the rest. He seemed the runt of the siblings, the outsider in the family, and that endeared him to Christie immediately.

He was also the perfect colour. Pedigree Great Danes come in a number of shades and patterns, and the different types of marking make a real difference in the show world. There are harlequins and brindles, merles and mantles, and then the pure colours, like black and fawn and blue. If your Great Dane is a pure colour, there must be no other colour fur on it anywhere. None of this mattered to me in the least. A puppy was a puppy was a puppy to my mind. But to Christie, being a girl (though I wasn't stupid enough to say that), colour did matter. She had her heart set on a blue one.

Happily, our little outsider was just that. In fact, he was blue as blue could be. His fur was almost the exact same steely blue as his eyes, and he had no white on him at all, which was very rare.

'Oh, Dave,' she cooed. 'Look at that one! That one's *sooo* cute! Let's see if she can send a bigger picture.'

The woman kindly obliged, sending through a whole stream of photos, and she confirmed that the one we'd picked, which she called 'the cute runt', was one of the six puppies left for sale. It seemed like an omen and we straight away agreed arrangements for her to ship the puppy from Oregon to Phoenix by air.

On the road trip up from Tucson to Phoenix — a journey of some two hours — Christie was pretty excited, and I knew, despite my initial reluctance to become a dog owner, that this had been the right thing to do. The only nagging doubt was about the timing, as I also knew that, because of our respective jobs, the day-to-day business of looking after our new pet would be a burden that would mostly fall on me.

Christie worked as a sales executive for a big medical equipment company, which meant she spent a lot of time on the road, visiting clients. It wasn't the sort of situation that worked well with a puppy, as there was no way she could take him along with her. I, on the other hand, worked for myself. These days I was a realtor, buying and fixing up houses for rental, which meant I was my own boss and could do what I liked — well, at least within *reason* I could do what I liked. I knew Christie figured that me taking a puppy to work came under the banner of 'hey, no big deal'. Personally, I wasn't so sure about that, but this was the plan we'd agreed on, this puppy, and I knew my wife couldn't wait to meet him. It would be just fine, I told myself, as we made our way north to pick up the newest member of our little family.

'So,' said Christie, as we headed up the

interstate. 'What are we going to call this pup of ours?'

What to call him wasn't something I'd given a whole lot of thought to. I was much more concerned with what we were going to *do* with him than with naming him. But she was excited and I knew I had to make an effort to be too. 'I dunno,' I said, trying to think on the hoof. 'How about something like . . . erm . . . Biggie?'

She laughed out loud at this — real loud. '*Biggie?*' she spluttered. 'What kind of a mad name is *that*?' She shook her head. She seemed to find my suggestion funny.

I didn't think I'd ever fully understand women and their foibles. What the hell was wrong with Biggie for a dog? 'It's a good name!' I countered, though, in truth, it really wasn't. I imagined calling it in a park: 'C'mon, Biggie! Biggie, here!' Nope. Biggie sucked.

'He'll be big,' I added anyway. 'You know. He's gonna be a big dog. So we call him Biggie. What's wrong with that? It's logical, isn't it? C'mon. It *is*! Or, I don't know, Fido, or Pluto? Or . . . hell, I don't *know*!'

She laughed again. '*Pluto?* Come *on*, hon. No. I think he should have a man's name. I like dogs with men's names.'

She'd obviously decided already, I realised.

17

'What?' I asked her. 'You mean something like Richard?'

She pulled a face. 'No, stupid. Something more . . . you know. More . . . ' She paused. 'I know!' she said finally. 'How about George?'

'George?'

'Yes. George is a cool name. You like George?'

I tried the park-calling thing again. It worked way, way better. 'George! C'mon here, George!' Yep, I thought. George I could do. 'Okay,' I said. 'Suits me. We'll call him George, then, shall we?'

'Yes,' agreed Christie. 'I think George is perfect — as long as he *looks* like a George when we see him.'

I wasn't sure quite what set of features would indicate this, but I knew better than to waste time trying to figure it out. 'Fine,' I said. 'If he looks like a George, then that's what we'll call him.'

And at no point did either of us think — hand on heart — about how easily you could prefix that with Giant . . .

★ ★ ★

We'd been given a bunch of instructions for what we had to do when we arrived at the airport in Phoenix. We had to go and collect him, apparently, from some special zone where they offload and deal with all the freight.

Once we'd found the right desk, and explained what we'd come for, we were then escorted through many doors and along several corridors, heading right into the bowels of the airport, to a strange silent area we'd never seen before. It was here, along with a woman who was picking up a cat, that we waited for the luggage cart to arrive that would be carrying the seven-week-old puppy.

The woman explained to us that she was waiting for her new pet, who was being flown in from LA, and that cats were also a big part of her working life.

'I own a pet modelling agency in Phoenix,' she told us, 'so I tend to be down here quite a lot.'

'Wow,' Christie said. 'That sounds like an interesting occupation. What kinds of animals do you represent?'

'Oh, all sorts . . . dogs, cats, the odd reptile here and there . . . What are you two picking up today? A cat too?'

Christie shook her head. 'Our new puppy,' she answered. 'A Great Dane.'

'Oh, good choice. I've got a couple on my books. Magnificent animals. And if he ever fancies strutting his stuff at any time, here — ' She plucked a small card from her bag. 'And, oh, here they are!' she added, looking beyond us. 'Arrived safe and sound. Aww . . . so cute!'

Her crate was handed over first, with ours right behind it, but all we could see at first was a stuffed animal, a rubber bone and two dishes, one of food and one of water. But then, behind all that, cowering on a crumpled grey blanket, was the puppy we'd decided to make ours. Christie opened the crate door and reached in to lift him out. He was just seventeen pounds and clearly terrified. What a journey it must have been for such a tiny animal! How must it have been for him, not only to have left his mother but then to be stuffed into a crate and put in the hold of an aircraft? We figured they must have heating — at that altitude, the animals would surely die if they didn't — but even so, it must have been one hell of an ordeal for him, all alone up there, probably in the dark.

He was no more than a tiny trembling ball of peach-fuzz blue fur, with four comically large paws at each corner. It must have been almost like a second birth, of sorts. Blinking in the harsh glare of the florescent airport lighting, he teetered to a standing position on our outstretched hands and moved his head slowly from side to side, taking in the wonder of it all. Then, finally, as if weighing us up and finding us okay, he tentatively snouted forward and gave Christie her first lick. We agreed he was the cutest little thing either of us had ever seen.

And he was ours now. 'So,' I asked Christie, as she cooed at him and petted him, 'what's the verdict? Does he look like a George?'

She paused in her stroking and considered him for a moment, tilting her head to one side. 'Hmm,' she said thoughtfully. 'I need to look carefully. Let me see now . . . ' The puppy looked back at her, bewildered.

'You know what?' she said finally. 'He does. He *really* does.' So that was that. George he would be.

We topped up his water bowl and placed him back in his crate for the long journey home, but not before the woman, who'd just done the same with her new kitten, had a chance to have a quick stroke as well.

'He's gorgeous,' she agreed with us. 'Absolutely gorgeous. And I tell you what,' she added, '*big* paws.'

Naturally, this didn't mean a lot to us. All we could see was this cute little puppy. Who knew that one day he'd be doing what she'd suggested — strutting his stuff for the whole *world* to see? Right now he just looked plain old bewildered.

21

★ ★ ★

Once we got back to the car, Christie changed her mind about George travelling home in the crate on the back seat. She decided he'd probably had enough of being stuck in a tiny box, and would much prefer to sit up front with his new mom.

'I'll travel with him on my lap,' she announced, and that was exactly what she did. She pulled him out of the crate again, cooing at him all the time and stroking him really gently, and soon his trembling began to stop. In fact, by the time we had reached the outskirts of Phoenix, he'd evidently started feeling so at home with his new mom that he decided to mark his territory.

'Guess what,' Christie said, as we reached the big highway, 'little George here appears to have peed in my lap.'

We both laughed, of course, because, well, it was pretty funny. But I also couldn't stop myself from thinking, 'Here we go ... ' Everything that had worried me about becoming a dog owner, would now, quite possibly, come true.

I didn't say that, though, because I didn't want to be a killjoy. Two were now three. We were committed.

2

Things That Go 'Bark' In The Night

It's obviously one thing to cheerfully adopt a good guy, wife-pleasing persona, but quite another to actually live it. Much as I had committed to this novel idea of being responsible for the welfare of a small dependent being, maybe I hadn't properly thought through the small print. We returned to our apartment with our seventeen-pound puppy, and it soon became obvious the reality of having him would require a heck of a lot more from me than the set of good intentions I'd committed to.

Right off the bat, it became clear that an unbroken night's sleep was something we could wave goodbye to. Like many a control freak before me, I suspect, I had a set of rules loosely in place. The first of these — and it wasn't at all unreasonable, I thought — was that George would sleep in his crate in the kitchen. He was a dog, after all, not a baby.

Three things immediately derailed this plan. The first was that we had figured things wrong. We had this idea that we could pretty much put him in his crate, leave him there and he'd go to sleep. This turned out to be seriously wishful thinking. As soon as we were out of sight — even before we'd left the kitchen — he'd start whimpering at the top of his lungs. He'd change instantly from being this cute little fella with blue eyes and winning ways to a caterwauling banshee from Hades. It wasn't that his howls and whines were demonic, exactly, just that they were high-pitched, interminable and super-loud. To sleep through his noise would probably require both earplugs and hard drugs, and even then I had a hunch it would still wake you.

The second problem, given our sleepless condition, was that the sort of parenting skills we'd sort of thought we'd possessed turned out to be impossible to apply. It was astonishing to me — if not to Christie, who was turning out to be naturally maternal — that even though George was not a human baby, there was something about the woeful, intense tone of his whining that made it impossible to ignore him. Every whimper we heard created a picture in our heads of a tragic, abandoned pup, left unloved and alone, desperate for the comfort of his mother. It didn't matter how much we rationalised things (warm crate, warm blanket, warm kitchen, squeaky bone), there was still a huge discrepancy between his quite comfortable situation in our nice warm kitchen and the aural fiction he was peddling so well.

'Poor, poor little thing,' Christie said on our second night into this torture. 'He must feel so bewildered. He's so young, after all. One minute he's snuggled up with his mother and all his brothers and sisters, and the next he's miles from home, feeling wretched, lost, abandoned . . . '

I didn't try to argue with this. I didn't bother commenting that he was a domestic pet; this was *normal*. What was the point? George's misery was eating at me, too.

So the sensible parenting was very soon dumped. Instead, we shunted George's crate into our bedroom, putting it close to our bed so he could see us. And that's where he slept from then on — though, to be fair to us, it wasn't *just* because we wimped out. The third problem, and, as it turned out, the biggest, was that the noise he made really was something. It was so loud that we didn't doubt for a single minute that we weren't the only ones who could hear it. We lived in an apartment, which meant people on all sides of us. Even if the folks living beneath us didn't hear him, chances were that the folks above would. And then there were the people to the left of us, and to the right of us

... Surely someone, in some apartment, would.

This was a problem in itself, because if that someone told the landlords we had a dog in our apartment, there were potentially serious consequences. No, we wouldn't be sent to an enforced labour camp in Siberia, or even run out of town by an angry (if quieter) posse, but we'd be breaking the terms of our lease and could find George and ourselves being given notice to leave — either move out or find George a new home. And it wouldn't just be that we'd be asked to leave, either. I checked the documents. They could make us move and *still* demand we pay the rent for the whole period. They could even take us to court — it could all get very ugly.

To make matters worse, George didn't confine his histrionics to the night-time. He would whimper and howl just about *any time* we left him, even for a half-hour or so. And we didn't simply guess this; we knew it. We knew because we both got so stressed about it happening that we checked for ourselves. One day, to be sure, we left the apartment without him, then waited right outside the door till his noise started up. Sure enough, within moments he was scratching at the door and barking, throwing in the odd howl for good measure. The noise was *loud*. We headed off,

26

then, to check round the back. The noise was still loud, and no less so when we went down to the courtyard. This puppy of ours could make noise for America. It was obvious there was no way we could leave him at home alone for any length of time, even had we wanted to, which we didn't.

We should have known about this, of course. One thing about the breed that was on almost every website Christie had visited was that Great Danes like — and really need — to be with their 'pack'. All the things that make them great pets — their lack of aggression, their attachment to their humans, their ability to seem to be able to read their owners' minds and act accordingly — also made them more emotionally sensitive than many other kinds of dog. These were dogs — and I'd read it myself too, more than once — that physically needed to be with you. And they really, *really* hated being left alone.

You take these things in, of course, but, like most things in life, you don't know what they truly mean until you're in that situation. And now we were in a situation where it was daily becoming clearer that leaving this puppy of ours wasn't an option. It wasn't simply a case of him coming to work with me sometimes, or of it being okay for us to pop out for a bite to eat. Nope, this puppy wanted in, *whatever* we were doing, whether it was a good place for a puppy to be or not.

So that was it. George became my workmate, my sidekick. And, initially, it wasn't too bad; it was do-able. Around the time we got him, I'd begun fixing up a property I'd bought in the south side of Tucson. It was a three bed, one bath home, in an inexpensive neighbourhood, that needed a lot of renovation. As well as painting and carpeting, landscaping and air-conditioning work, it had an add-on room that needed to be completely rebuilt. And since I was working there mostly alone, there wouldn't be any problems if I brought George along . . . or so I thought. I hadn't factored in Nosy Rosie.

We didn't know if Rosie was her name; it probably wasn't. But even before we'd crossed the line on pet-owning issues, she pretty much fit the bill. She lived on the ground floor of our apartment building and clearly needed to get out more. As it was, she didn't seem to want to. In fact, she didn't seem much interested in any kind of socialising — all she seemed to do was constantly peer through the slats in her blinds, checking out her fellow residents' comings and goings, presumably in case any of us were felons.

Neither Christie nor I had spoken with her much, but it was clear from the start that she had our movements in her sights. This meant the business of sneaking George in and out of the building needed to be a covert military operation. We knew — we just *knew* — Nosy Rosie would be the type to log our movements and report them to our landlord.

For the first couple of weeks, it wasn't too bad. I'd sneak him out, in his crate, cleverly disguised under a blanket, and, similarly, when he needed to use the bathroom before bedtime, I'd take him out the same way and walk down the road until I could safely let him out to do his thing.

After two weeks, however, he'd already put on another fourteen pounds, which meant the crate was no longer big enough to take him. I decided to upgrade to a stout cardboard box, and would furtively carry him, in the manner of an illicit package, to wherever it was he and I needed to be.

He couldn't remain illicit for too long, however. As with the separation anxiety, the question of George's growth was something we knew about, had read about, had definitely expected, but the reality of it came as something of a shock. As he grew — and, boy, was he growing — so did the effort required to carry him. Why hadn't I figured on that before? And it wasn't just a case of carrying him, either; I had to carry him downstairs and outside while *at the same time* locking doors, manoeuvring handles and unlocking truck tailgates. It wasn't long before I had to abandon the box and simply gather him up under my arm, again covered in a blanket, like a convicted criminal on his way to court. What George thought of all this was anyone's guess, but, knowing no different, and being such a personable and enthusiastic animal, my hunch is that he found it all pretty neat.

But I was getting seriously fed up with it. It wasn't just the journey to work and back that was beginning to prove stressful, nor the cover-of-darkness trips to go poop, all the while looking out for Nosy Rosie and wondering when the landlord would come a-knocking; it was a complete nightmare when I was *at* work as well. How had I ever convinced myself it wouldn't be?

While Christie had settled in well in her new job, and would come home full of tales of the interesting people she'd met over dinner at work functions, the clients she'd acquired and the out-of-town trips she had to make, I was beginning to get behind schedule, as I had to spend half my day shepherding an inquisitive ball of energy with a voracious appetite in order to get anything done.

In the past when I was working I'd always gone off to have a leisurely lunch somewhere — to a local sandwich shop or deli. It was a good way to break up my mostly solitary day, because I could see people, chat to them and socialise a bit. But this was obviously no longer an option. I couldn't take George with me because dogs weren't allowed in restaurants, nor could I leave him at the house I was remodelling. What if somebody took him? The house was completely unsecured. And I didn't know any of the neighbours. Even if I did risk leaving him somewhere, he'd start yowling.

So it was all a bit gloomy, and lonely, for both of us. Because I couldn't leave him, I couldn't get to the store to get parts for the heating and air conditioning, so I would spend each day pretty much in solitary confinement. We'd eat the lunches I now had to prepare and pack every morning — turkey sandwiches and chips for me, and puppy food for him — indoors, out of the 40-degree heat that was the norm for spring. And then I'd get back to work and leave George in another room, unable to relax for a second for fear that he'd either find a way to escape or chew through an electrical cord or something.

I considered the yard, too. It was large — a

big patch of dirt — and it was empty. It was still cool enough outdoors (40 degrees in Arizona is nothing compared to how hot it *can* get in the summer) that spending a short time outside wouldn't hurt him. But the house was a mess both inside and out, and the yard was a minefield of potential puppy problems. There was no swimming pool for him to fall into, but there were plenty of other hazards, from the shards of broken glass to the stray nails in bits of lumber and the scorpions that might decide to stop by. But the greatest hazard, in my view, was the cat poop — there were *dozens* of cat poops — and I knew he'd probably want to try some. But he'd not yet been inoculated, and wouldn't be for a few weeks, so he could catch any number of horrible diseases. It didn't escape my notice that a dog with diarrhoea and sickness would make my already stressful life a good deal more so. He really shouldn't even have been out in public yet.

If I was being brutally honest, I thought to myself darkly, this puppy of ours shouldn't have been *bought* yet. We should have done the sensible thing and left Project Puppy till Christie had got herself settled in her new job, and we'd found ourselves a house to live in.

It took about three weeks for the problems with George to come to a head: three weeks in which the problems of looking after him not only failed to get easier to deal with but, day by day, they simply got worse.

It wouldn't become entirely clear to us for a couple of years yet, but our puppy, who'd started out the size of, say, a six-month-old baby, was growing at an absolutely incredible rate. By early March he had, literally, doubled in size. He was only about fourteen weeks old — still a baby — yet he already weighed thirty-four pounds. Thirty-four pounds is an awful lot of puppy, especially if that puppy is living his life incognito and needs to be carried in and out secretly.

It was obvious his days of going anywhere in a crate were over, as thirty-four pounds of puppy takes one hell of a lot of lifting, but he still needed a crate for use at home. We'd researched it, and it seemed that crate-training a dog — particularly a large one — was pretty much considered essential. You needed to have a place where you could safely park your mutt during times when he'd be in your way. At this point the notion of 'being in your way' was one we were only just encountering — the full impact would come a bit later — but he certainly needed a place to sleep. So I spent a good bit of time researching various dog crates, and I found one — the biggest dog crate then available on the market, which was appropriately called the 'Colossus'.

The spec for the Colossus was pretty impressive. '54″ long, 37″ wide, 45″ tall — or 137 cm long, 94 cm wide, 114 cm tall', said the package. It also said it would be good for large dogs — up to one hundred and fifty pounds. Perfect, I thought. That should last us pretty well. An adult male Great Dane, I remembered from my research, weighed in at around that weight, didn't he?

When our Colossus arrived, it took the UPS man three separate trips to get all of it into our apartment, which set Rosie's curtains a-twitching. We assembled and set it up in the corner of our bedroom. It was some piece of furniture: it was *enormous*. If I'd had any lingering notions that we might move it with George in it, they were, in that moment, dispelled.

It was also perhaps that day (or the next one, if not) when it occurred to me that I was at the end of my rope — I was stressed out and cranky and getting snappy with poor Christie. It felt like the whole thing had been *her* big idea, yet I was the one with all the headaches. I couldn't help feeling resentful, however much I wished I didn't, that I was dealing with so much stress and inconvenience, whereas she could come home from work and pet him and have fun.

This was *all* utter madness. I had really had enough, and I couldn't get the irritation out of my head. It had been a mad idea, clearly. It wasn't that I was against having a dog — we'd agreed that — but to get this kind of dog, and at this time, felt wrong.

And once the idea took root, it quickly gained strength; it drilled a taproot right in and began to flourish. Yes, we'd been looking at houses, but we were a long way from finding one, let alone buying and moving into one. In the meantime, was it fair on either of us, not to mention George, to live daily with all this hassle and tension?

It wasn't fair on any of us. It wasn't practical. It wasn't sensible. And, most of all, I'd discovered — however much I hated to admit it — everything about owning a dog had become one big 24/7 problem.

And the problem was growing. It wasn't that I didn't like George — he was a cute guy, he was funny. It wasn't his fault he drove me nuts. But this wasn't going to get any easier; it would only get harder. With every pound he put on, my resolve grew a little stronger.

There was no balance here — not like there would be one day with kids. You went through all the stress with babies, or so my raddled thinking went, but then they grew up and became . . . well, grown up, I supposed. It was *worth* it. Everyone knew it was worth it. But this? Well, I wasn't sure this was. I felt like an ass, but I had really had enough.

'Christie,' I admitted one night, when we both got home from work. 'I can't do this any more. I really can't.'

Her expression told me everything her silence didn't. She put her bag down on the counter and regarded me coolly, in much the same way as a teacher might look at a student who's disappointed her, who's failed her, who's let her down.

Seeing Christie's reaction, I felt even more of an ass. After all, I'd made a promise. And this was a puppy who was very much Christie's baby, even if I did do all the day care. She'd really thrown herself into being a mom to him, too. Hell, he already had his own photo album and growth chart up and running — as if we needed reminding. Reading it, we'd stand there and gawp in awe.

I opened the fridge and pulled out a soft drink for her. 'Aren't you going to say something?' I asked her.

She took the drink and shrugged her

shoulders. 'What's the point?' she answered. 'It's not like it's going to make any difference to things, is it? You've obviously made up your mind . . . '

She didn't need to go on. I knew exactly what she meant. We were both strong-willed, both stubborn, both keen to get our way. And she knew me better than anyone. Once I was set on something, I couldn't often be shifted from doing it. But I was still surprised. This mattered to her, didn't it? Mattered a lot. So why wasn't she trying to change my mind?

I asked her.

'Because I don't want us to do something that doesn't make you happy,' she said simply. 'If I try to talk you out of this, what happens next? You resent him, that's what. *And* me, for making you keep him when you don't want to. And that won't work, will it?' She picked up her bag and put down her drink. 'So if your mind's really set, honey, then I guess you'd better go ahead and find him a new home.'

I think that 'honey' was the lowest point of all.

3

Home, Sweet Home

As low points go, the evening I told Christie I wanted to get rid of George still ranks as pretty low indeed.

Obviously I felt wretched about it all. I had reneged on a promise. I had proven myself to be not up to scratch as a husband, and I had exhibited the sort of devotion to selfish pleasures that made me feel like a real ass. But after I'd made the decision to keep him, and made the calls to those disappointed people who had answered the ad and wanted him, and apologised to him and to Christie, I felt great. I felt like I'd stepped up to the plate as a man. I even felt a tiny bit heroic. My commitment to keeping George — keeping him willingly, not grudgingly — was something that made me feel a whole lot better about myself.

As luck would have it, fortune was kind to us; only a week after I'd let down the people from the small ad, we finally found the perfect house — not that it would have appeared perfect to many people. It was a 'fixer': a house that needed a lot of renovation, and would prove difficult to live in for many, many months. But having been holed up in a rented apartment with an illegal, and rapidly expanding, puppy, any house with a yard, however dilapidated and sad looking, would feel like the palace of our dreams.

Finally, we were going to make a proper home in Tucson, and it felt like the right time, the right place, the right everything. Sure California had plenty to offer, but our corner of Arizona was a pretty neat place as well.

Since I'd left it, my home town had grown a lot, and it now has nearly a million residents. In fact, one of the best lures I'd hoped to use on Christie was that this place, once a dusty desert town full of cacti and cowboys, had — and still has — some great malls and theatres and plenty to do. It's also, by any yardstick, beautiful.

For a time a part of Mexico (Tucson joined the USA only in 1854), the city sits amid five separate mountain ranges, where the cacti (this is Arizona — we still have a *lot* of cacti) form eye-popping spiky forests in the foothills. It's also iconic: right after it became a part of the US, the ranchers, settlers and miners who flooded in clashed badly with the indigenous Indian populations — the Apaches — putting Tucson at the very heart of the bloodbath that was the 'Wild West'.

There would be no more clashes with the locals for Christie and George and me, though. We waved goodbye to Nosy Rosie and to the hassle and the headaches of subterfuge, packed up all our stuff, including the Colossus, and moved into our new home in February 2006.

The house we'd fallen in love with was a sprawling single-storey property, situated in a pretty residential part of the north-east of the city, in an area where friends of mine from high school already lived. It was the kind of place where you knew the owners took pride in their homes; all the yards were well manicured and the homes looked well cared for. It seemed like a nice place to put down some roots.

In the middle of all this stood a house — our new home — that looked like it needed some loving. The previous owner had kept his motorcycle parked in the living room and the oil from it had badly stained the carpet. It also had a 1960s chrome Fabulous 400 model oven/cook-top, which would have had that real 'wow' factor when it was installed fifty years ago, and was, if you were into that kind of thing, a real antique. Though it might have sounded fabulous — if a little quaint — to an enthusiast, the house was basically old and dirty.

And it wasn't just the house either: the front yard had an extended family of rats in the bushes, and there were numerous moving boxes littered everywhere. It had a leaky roof, dodgy plumbing, take-your-life-in-your-hands electricals, and the interior air hummed with the smell of pet urine. The front yard fountain was in disrepair and no longer worked, and the trees and bushes, lacking both water and care, were on their last legs, and were being choked by all the weeds, which were thriving. It looked not so much a home as a Walt Disney backdrop for the sort of horror ride that had everyone terrified before they started at the very thought of what dreadful sights and events might be in store for them. Undaunted by the dramatic visuals, however, we immediately set about making plans for it.

We'd decided it was perfect for many reasons. Being right in the centre of town, the location was obviously highly desirable, but at the same time it felt quiet and residential. The whole place was green and pretty, with big mature trees, plenty of flowers and open spaces. It was also on a cul de sac, well away from big busy streets, so it was great place for kids to get outside and ride bikes. Best of all, though, was that the lot the house stood on was large, allowing freedom for George to run around and have fun, and there was space for my grand home demolition and construction plans.

But grand plans of any kind require time and commitment, and though I was about as committed as could be, time was something I was a little short on. Having persuaded Christie of my credentials as a brilliant home-remodeller, right away I fell short in terms of actually getting on and doing it. By now I had almost finished work on my first rental property in Tucson, and had already started work on a new one, so it was difficult to balance the demands of creating our new 'dream house' with all the ongoing rental property work. Naturally, the rental properties were getting most of my attention, since this was the way I was earning my living, but, clearly, this wasn't making Christie happy. This wasn't because she didn't understand and support me in my work, but because it was taking so long and she wanted this bedraggled house of ours to begin to feel like our home.

Here we were, living in an oil-stained, weed-infested dump of a place with an antique kitchen, a dilapidated bathroom and no light at the end of the tunnel. We'd created a tiny makeshift sleeping space out of one of the original bedrooms, and into it crammed our bed and George's Colossus crate, which, between them, left barely enough room to walk in and out of the door.

During the construction work, we obviously had to remodel the kitchen too, which meant moving our temporary kitchen — essentially a microwave and refrigerator — into the other little bedroom, and it occurred to me (I didn't like to dwell on this too much) that the conditions were more cramped and unsuitable than they'd been in the apartment we'd just left.

But, despite all, I was happy. It didn't matter how difficult and tiny our living quarters were, I was loving it. I loved fixing up houses; it was work that made me happy. I was finally doing the job I felt suited me best, even if I'd taken my time getting to it. After leaving college, I'd done a whole bunch of things, but I'd spent the last decade making a living in retail. I'd set up a small business — a health food store in Long Beach, California — and enjoyed a fruitful ten years expanding, setting up five more stores in Southern California. I'd done okay, and on the whole had enjoyed running my business, but perhaps I'd always known that it wouldn't be forever. I wasn't afraid of hard work (I thrived on it, mostly), but there was a real seven-days-a-week culture — as there always is in retailing — and additional responsibility for an ever-growing team of staff.

Deep down, I knew I needed a new venture. It had been selling my shops over a period of eighteen months that had given me the capital to buy the first property in Tucson. It had been logical to base my new plan in Arizona, because the price differential between there and California was substantial, and I knew my investment in property there would give great returns.

I loved that our new home was a place where we could make our own mark, set down some roots, build it the way *we* wanted it to be (if a little slowly . . .) and create a proper family home — not that I was up for doing the family bit *quite* yet. We'd been married no time at all; we were still finding our feet, and moving into our first proper home was just one step along that road. We needed to get settled, make friends, get to know our new neighbourhood — and perhaps get to know each other a little better too. I was also very conscious that though this was my home town, and to me felt familiar and easy, it was new territory for Christie.

It had been a pretty big deal for Christie to agree to come here with me, away from the beach, away from all the fantastic restaurants and the huge choice of shops that were right on our doorstep in LA. Most of all, it had been no small sacrifice for Christie to move away from her family and friends. Sure, she got along just fine with my family, and they adored her, but was that enough? I hated to think she might be lonely in Tucson, and I was worried she didn't have the kind of job where she'd be likely to find many new girlfriends. She worked in a mostly male-dominated industry: her company had over 800 sales reps nationally, and Christie was one of only eight women. She was on the road most of the time, meeting with clients, and though her clients were friendly, they were clients, not pals.

The more I thought about it, the more I realised what a stupid thing I'd done even *suggesting* we give George away. She needed her puppy every bit as much as he needed his mom. I resolved to keep that in mind at all times.

Our puppy no longer looked much like a puppy, though. He clearly was one — he still acted like a puppy, turning circles to chase his tail, playing endless games of fetch, as well as tug-of-war with his favourite bit of rope, out in the backyard. In fact, he was about the most playful puppy you could find. But at just five months old George was already the weight and size of a fully grown Labrador. When we'd moved into the house, he'd weighed fifty-three pounds, and since then, in just a month, he'd put on another twenty-four, which meant an average gain of just under a pound a *day*. It was unbelievable to think that George was now a whopping seventy-seven pounds. And it wasn't just Christie and I who were amazed at his growth rate: our new veterinarian, William Wallace, was too.

'For his age,' he'd told me, right off the bat, when George and I went to meet him for the first time, 'that's the biggest Great Dane puppy I've ever seen.'

And he'd certainly seen a few in his time, because Doc Wallace was a respected large breed specialist. He was very well known in the dog-owning community, and had been practising for four decades. He was in his late sixties, but still had a full head of blond hair, and you could see he was in pretty good shape. He was a colourful character, and easy to spot too, because he had a fondness for wearing plaid pants. He'd been recommended to us by a number of people, including professionals who worked in the pet health care industry, so it wasn't just his charm that made us choose him as our vet — his reputation was impressive.

Doc Wallace ran an office and surgical facility ten minutes from our house, and towards the end of April I headed over to see him to get George fixed up with whatever inoculations he needed so we could start getting him out and about.

There were also a whole load of questions I needed to have answered, as Great Danes, like any other specialist breed of animal, come with their own set of unique challenges. One of these was their potential, given their great size, for having serious problems with their hips. Happily, that potential could at least in part be spotted after a simple examination when the dog was still a puppy.

George (and I would come to realise this was also the case with almost all the dogs our veterinarian saw) took to Doc Wallace right away, and wasted no time in making his admiration felt, by wagging his tail and leaning his ever-growing frame against the Doc's legs. George loved to lean against people he liked: it was one of his favourite ways of feeling close. It's a real Great Dane thing, this love of leaning up against people. As it turned out — understandably, I guess — George's affection would slowly begin to dissipate as he made more visits to the vet, as soon as he realised that going to Doc Wallace's would invariably mean lots of poking and prodding and needles.

But when George liked you, you knew about it. Now he was getting bigger, his displays of affection could have you pinned temporarily against a wall or a piece of furniture. It was his version of a bear-hug.

Straight off you could see that our vet had a gift. It seemed he could do almost anything to an animal without it getting angry and growling or biting. I'm not sure I'd have reacted with such grace and equanimity had a man in plaid pants laid *me* down on my back and immediately splayed my hind legs, even if it *was* to investigate my hip joints. But George didn't so much as huff at him. And his hips, the doc confirmed, seemed just fine.

'But you'll need to get him neutered,' he told me, as he righted George. 'And it's important that we do it at the right time,' he added, 'because if it's left too long, it can result in his bones not fusing properly and then over-growing, which could give him all sorts of other problems.' I assured him that that's what we'd do. 'And at the same time,' he explained, 'we can do his gastropexy — that way he's only under the anaesthetic the one time.'

The gastropexy, he explained, was an operation to staple George's stomach to the inside lining of his abdominal wall to prevent something nasty called bloat from happening. Bloat is a well-recognised problem with large breeds — most commonly in Great Danes — due to their size and the dimensions of their chests, and is caused by a build-up of swallowed air in the stomach.

Swallowing air when stressed is very common in Great Danes. They tend to do it most when they're feeling anxious, and that happens when they lack company. They're not great dogs to get if you're going to be away working all day, because they really do hate to be left alone, as we were well aware.

Bloat not only creates pressure on the surrounding organs, it can also lead to the stomach flipping over on itself and cutting off its own blood supply. It's dangerous if that happens, as it can kill a dog in hours; even with professional intervention and treatment, around thirty per cent of dogs with bloat die. The gastropexy, therefore, was a sensible option, especially since he was going under for his sterilisation anyway. It might also take his mind off an even more distressing scenario: having some human, however friendly he appeared on the surface, put him under and then cut off his manhood. It was just as well George didn't know what we were talking about right then, or I swear he'd have bolted for the mountains.

A more sensible option still, and I remember this did cross my mind as George and I left the vet's office, would have been not to have a Great Dane in the first place, given this huge potential for heartache that came with them. Like many large dogs, their life span wasn't that long: anything over about seven or eight years was pretty good going for a Dane — something we'd known from the outset. But now I had a bunch of new pictures in my mind of the horrible things that could go wrong with our pet — the potential for hip problems and the dreaded bloat — which could take his life at an even earlier age.

For the moment, however, George was pronounced fit and well, and as fine a specimen of a Great Dane puppy as the doc had ever seen. And, as I pointed out to Christie that evening, so far — given his current growth rate — the biggest . . .

★ ★ ★

Once George had begun his inoculations and was free to socialise with other dogs, we were finally able to unleash him on the world and let him explore a little further afield. Since there was a dog park not too far from where we lived, it made sense to go and acquaint ourselves with it.

But first up, being responsible parents, we decided we should get him a little training. Christie had seen puppy-training classes advertised at the pet store we usually used to buy our ever-expanding supplies of puppy food, so she signed up to join some group classes.

George proved himself to be a model pupil, and took to the training with real enthusiasm. The system was based on Pavlovian-style conditioning, using clickers to reinforce various commands. He took to it easily, soon learned the commands 'sit', 'stay', 'down' and so on, and graduated from class in no time. However, Christie felt, as he was such a large breed of animal, some private tutoring would be beneficial too.

We'd chosen a Great Dane partly because they are temperamentally quiet, well-behaved pets, but we'd also read that they could be emotionally fragile if not properly trained from the start, and this could lead to them becoming difficult to manage. We had no idea at this point just how big George was going to get, but it made sense if you were going to have a big animal in your home to train that animal to obey you at all times — not to do so would have been irresponsible.

So George had five sessions of training with a private dog trainer, and he loved every minute of that too. The private trainer used something called a 'pinch collar', which looks, if you don't know about them, like an instrument of torture, as it's a chain-link collar with blunt spikes at regular intervals that face inwards, towards the dog's neck, but it's actually much kinder than a choke collar. Whereas the choke collar does pretty much what its name suggests and constricts the throat, the pinch collar simply gets the dog's attention, making the process of getting him to know his place in your 'pack' much quicker to establish. And since the key to having happy dogs is for them to know where they stand, we felt the training was money well spent.

With the help of the pinch collar, our boisterous boy became, once again, a model pupil. So we were done. Our ball of cuddly blue fuzz had come a long way since we'd picked him up from the Phoenix airport. As well as being bigger — and, *boy*, was he getting bigger — he was also confident, socialised, obedient and good to go. He was ready to meet the world, play and make some new doggie friends.

We just had no idea how tricky that was going to turn out to be.

4

It's a Jungle Out There

Like any new parents who dote on their baby, we thought George was lovely — the perfect family pet. Okay, so that may be a little bit of an overstatement, to be honest, since he was still big, and getting bigger, and chowing down huge amounts of food, and making a mess, and doing poops, and taking over *the whole bed*, but even so he was a real nice puppy.

And like any new parents, when we started taking him to the dog park, we hoped everyone else would think he was a nice puppy too. Why wouldn't they? George was totally gorgeous.

I guess we just hadn't figured it out yet.

In Tucson there are several dog parks — places where people can take their pets to run around off the leash, play with other dogs and generally enjoy some down time together, safely away from any roads. Our nearest one was the Morris K. Udall Park, which was named after an esteemed Arizona politician, Morris King Udall, who'd served in the House of Representatives for thirty years. Morris was a bit of a local hero by all accounts. The state of Arizona was always at the forefront of championing the rights of Native American Indians anyway, and Morris, together with his brother, Stewart, was responsible for several political initiatives to support them. He was also an enthusiastic and committed environmentalist and saw through a lot of important legislation. It was a nice park; I'm sure he would have liked it.

The park was a five-minute drive from our new home, and was split into two big areas: an area for puppies and small dogs, up to around thirty pounds, and another area for adult and bigger dogs. Straight away this gave us a problem: George, at just a few months old, was still very much a puppy, but already weighed more than the maximum thirty pounds for the puppy area. Still, since he *was* a puppy, we figured he should be in the small dog area. After all, you wouldn't leave a young child in a schoolyard full of teenagers, would you? But right away, on our very first visit to the dog park, it appeared he wasn't welcome in the puppy part. Though he wasn't doing anything wrong — he was just doing what puppies do: running around, having fun, getting to know the other dogs — he was clearly the subject of disapproval.

'Did you hear that?' hissed Christie. She was sitting at one of the benches in the shade. I'd been throwing George's ball for him and had just sent it soaring. He galloped off to get it, and I sat down.

'Hear what?'

'What that woman over there said!'

'What woman over wh . . . '

'Shhh!' Christie whispered. She'll *hear* you!'

'Oh, right,' I said. 'Sorry.' I followed her gaze. 'What, *that* woman? The one in the green?'

'Yes, *that* woman. Her.'

'So what did she say?'

Christie moved her mouth a little closer to my ear. 'She pointed and she said, 'What are those folks doing, bringing *him* in here?' And then she shook her head. Look, there!' Christie now poked me in the ribcage. 'Look — see? She's pointing at him again!'

I rubbed my rib. 'Just ignore her. He's a puppy, so he has a perfect right to be here.'

She beckoned to George, who was galloping back with his prize. 'Hmmph,' she said, picking up the ball from where George had dropped it. '*She* obviously doesn't think so.'

'Well, that's just too bad. He isn't doing anything wrong.'

I took a look at her as Christie stood and hurled the ball into the air again. The woman's dog was small and well manicured — like a lawn, a bit like her 1980s haircut. The dog was white, and looked like it might be a Pomeranian. It also, I saw, had a bow in its hair.

The bow told me nothing, of course — absolutely nothing. But at the same time I really couldn't help but consider that . . . well, it *did* kind of figure. Would she, I wondered, view George a little more kindly if we'd taken the trouble to accessorise his head? But no, that was silly; it wouldn't make the slightest difference.

It was about then that the woman glanced in our direction, before turning back to the other owner she'd been chatting to, their conversation clearly still about George. George was still doing nothing other than playing with the other dogs and puppies, and, if anything, was doing so a little shyly. You could see that he was nervous about being there; he was actually a bit anxious about all the other dogs milling around him. With or without ribbons in their hair, they were still dogs, pack animals with a code of seniority, and among them, George was very much bottom dog. He looked to me about as threatening as a wet paper bag.

'You see!' said Christie again, indignant as any slighted mother.

'Ignore her,' I told her. 'George is doing nothing wrong. Besides, if she has something to say about him being here, then she should quit with all the whispering and pointing, and come over and say it to our faces.' I added a glare in her direction to display my solidarity, and decided that the best thing to do was to dismiss her as a silly, neurotic, over-anxious woman.

⋆　⋆　⋆

But what did *I* know? She clearly wasn't alone in her disapproval.

'That dog shouldn't be in here.'

It was only a couple of days later, and George and I were back in the dog park. This time the person was saying it to my face, and it wasn't the silly, neurotic, over-anxious woman. Well, he might have been some of those things, but he was definitely not a woman.

Since I was sitting and he was standing, I blinked up at him, shielding my eyes from the glare of the sun. 'Excuse me?'

'You shouldn't have your dog in here,' he went on. 'He's too big. This part's for small dogs. It says on the sign.'

I stood up. 'And puppies,' I pointed out, because I'd read the sign too. 'It's also the area for *puppies*. And he's a puppy. He's only just seven months old. He's too young to be in the adult dog area.'

'But he's too big to be in here,' the man said, clearly implacable. 'He could hurt other dogs by running into them — '

'Which he doesn't.'

'Or treading on them accidentally — '

'Which he doesn't do either.'

'But he might. C'mon, here! He's way, *way* too big. He should be — ' the guy pointed 'in *there*.'

But the truth was that far from hurting or intimidating any other dog, the exact opposite was what mostly happened. The smaller dogs would run both around him *and* under him, and he'd be constantly sidestepping them, obviously anxious and jittery, not to mention traumatised, as any sensitive guy would be, when some of the adult ones tried to hump his legs.

But it seemed our George, without doing anything to deserve it, had been cast in the role of social misfit. And, bowing to the pressure from other owners, which was becoming oppressive and difficult to deal with, after a few visits during which we took George to the puppy section, we decided that perhaps we'd better take heed of the comments and give him a try in the large dog enclosure instead.

At least there, we thought, he wouldn't stick out like a sore thumb, and as a big guy perhaps he would feel right at home. And maybe we wouldn't feel quite so stressed. It was no fun to sit there and feel everyone's eyes on us — even less when they started up with all the pointing.

How wrong we were. This was far worse. The fact is that whatever size a creature is, it's the maturity that is important, and with pack animals like dogs, this is key. George, however intimidating-looking people seemed to find him, was very much a puppy in the world of the adult dog enclosure, and right off the other dogs let him know that.

Whereas in the puppy part he'd struggled with his size and lack of confidence, here, even though his size didn't matter, he was bullied remorselessly from the start. He was constantly buffeted by other, older dogs, who made their authority clear by running fast and bumping into him, sniffing him aggressively and generally acting kind of mean. Any time we threw his ball or his beloved piece of rope for him, there was always sure to be some other dog who'd go haring after it, invariably, even if he didn't beat George to it, making it clear that he'd better keep back.

It was hard to police this — they were animals, just *being* animals — but a line had to be drawn, and one day, sure enough, it got crossed. We were at the dog park one lunch-time a few weeks later, when George was attacked by not one but two dogs at once. They were a pair of mixed-breed dogs, both smaller than George, but adult and obviously very confident.

We'd just arrived at the park that afternoon, and were walking towards the central area, when this guy came in with his two dogs. It all kicked off incredibly quickly. One minute all was quiet, and George was bounding around happily; the next thing I knew, a terrible commotion had started up, with that all too familiar — not to mention horrible — noise when a dog starts acting really aggressive.

I leapt up, but by the time I was over to the three animals, the first of the dogs was just about to bite George. The other was at his opposite flank, trying to do the same thing, and Georgie was whimpering and trembling uncontrollably. There was obviously no fight in this gentle giant of ours, but his lack of reaction or retaliation didn't seem to make any difference.

The other dogs' owner looked as shocked

by what was happening as I was. Though he repeatedly yelled at his animals to get off George, neither dog paid him the slightest bit of attention. In the end, it took brute force to drag the dogs off a now terrified George, the owner hauling one of his pets off by the collar, and then, having had no success in getting near the front end of his other dog, and no other option, yanking him off by his tail.

He looked mortified, and was very apologetic about it all, and immediately put his dogs back on their leashes. As for me, I'd been a dog 'dad' for such a short time, I had no idea what the appropriate etiquette was at times like this. As scared as I'd been of what might have happened to poor George, who was shaking, and cowering close at my side, I figured the whole thing must have come as a complete shock to the other guy as well, so I accepted his obviously sincere apology, and just hoped George didn't run into his two dogs again. The guy left the park right away.

I gave George a check-over, and no blood had been shed, but he was clearly bruised and very traumatised. His confidence, always tenuous, was shot to pieces, and it occurred to me that George had been bullied at the park only because we'd let a few dog owners in the puppy part bully us. We decided then and there that the adult park was not where he belonged yet, and began taking him back into the puppy and small dog part, determined to ignore the constant comments and glares from the other owners. The phrase 'pick on someone your own size' had a distinctly hollow ring. Our poor pup was a misfit, it seemed.

★ ★ ★

Ironically, it was only a few days after the incident in the adult dog section that a guy entered the park with a Great Dane. As dog owners do when they have pets in common, he came straight over to the chain-link fence that separated the big dogs from the smaller ones, beckoned to Christie and me and said, 'Hi'. His dog was called Drake, and was a handsome black Great Dane. He obviously also had a great temperament, like George's — you could see it. He was, his owner told us, about five years old. He seemed enormous to us, and, having become so preoccupied with George's size lately, we asked him how much Drake weighed.

'One hundred and forty pounds,' he said. We were both open-mouthed. Yes, George was pretty big, but we couldn't imagine him ever getting — ever being — *that* big. It seemed impossible, unthinkable, that George could get so huge.

I said so to Christie on the way home from the park. 'Still,' I added, 'if he gets anywhere near to that sort of weight, no dog's going to take him on — no way.'

She smiled. 'What d'you reckon, Georgie?' she said, reaching into the back seat of the truck to pet him. 'I think you need to grow some more, sweetie. Then you'll show 'em.'

I think somebody upstairs must have been listening.

5

Honey, I Shrunk The House

'You know what?' Christie said to me one day in early summer. 'I swear I can actually *see* Georgie growing.'

She'd taken to calling George 'Georgie' early on — not something that sat terribly well with me, it must be said. What guy wants to take his dog to the dog park and keep yelling the name 'Georgie' at him? But as he was still (if I was asked to say at gunpoint, at any rate) Christie's dog, I didn't feel I could intervene. And it wasn't even 'Georgie' either, girly though that was. She'd taken to pronouncing it 'Georg-eeee'.

But she was right. Though you obviously couldn't see it — that would be crazy — it was beginning to seem as if he'd go to sleep one size and wake up the next day a whole lot bigger. He'd outgrown what we'd thought was the not to be outgrown Colossus, and we'd given up the whole idea of even having a crate, since there was none — unless I attempted to knock one up myself — big enough for him to fit into. We'd progressed from the largest crate available *anywhere* to a single-sized bed mattress, which was positioned at the foot of our bed for him to sleep on. He still preferred to spend a chunk of the night curled up in bed *with* us, but if things got too uncomfortable — for George, that is, obviously; we, as parents, just had to deal with it — he'd happily stretch out on his own bed.

Christie had made the observation about George's amazing growth rate off the back of another conversation. She'd come in from work and was taking her shoes off while I told her how I'd seen George make a dent in a corner of the kitchen wall just by wagging his tail as he passed — unbelievable but true. We had the evidence of it happening, which we showed off to my folks when they called round, like a proud mom and pop showing off a kiddie's growth chart.

So it was doubly good that our house was part home and part building site: with your home in such a state, you tend not to get quite so annoyed if your enormous puppy inadvertently lays waste to all your stuff — not that we had much stuff lying around, in any case. Again, like parents with a toddler, we had soon cottoned on to the fact that our rapidly expanding mutt was still very much a juvenile and still behaved in mostly puppyish ways. He would bound around like Bambi, skittering on the newly laid — and very shiny, very slippy — wooden floors, hurling himself with boundless enthusiasm at everything he fancied, be it 'mom' — whom he adored — or a Ming vase. We weren't exactly Ming vase kinds of people, admittedly, but if we had been at any point, we sure wouldn't be any more.

As if sensing he was being talked about, George ambled up to Christie, got up on his hind legs and licked her on the face.

Dogs have amazing senses generally, of course, but it was evident that two of George's were fast becoming superior. Like all dogs, he was really good at hearing things we couldn't, and he had a highly developed sense of smell. George particularly loved the way his mom smelled, and, boy, was he was keen to let her know it. He would seek out and lick any single fragrant thing off her: her face cream, her perfume, her make-up, her body lotion — any trace of anything she put on her skin. George would lap it up like a cat laps up cream. And he could smell it from an incredibly long way away. She could put some stuff on in the bedroom and George, from, say, the backyard, would pick the scent up and come right along and lick her clean in an instant. If we were going out for the evening, she'd have to factor in extra minutes to dodge his attentions so she could get out unscathed.

What he most loved, however, was when she blowdried her hair. Christie wielding a hairdryer was nirvana to George, and would send him into raptures of excitement. Whereas some animals respond to the sound of a food can or packet being opened, George would canter to wherever the sound of the hairdryer was coming from. He was like a homing pigeon, and, once again, it was all about smell, about the way her hair, treated with whatever conditioner she'd been using, would fill the air around her with its scent.

On the other hand, although I had all the Brownie points for looking after George all day, I was also the bad guy — a lot. All I did — and I could see from George's eyes this really annoyed him — was to make a series of horrible, ear-splitting noises.

When George was with me when I was at work, which was most days, I was usually drilling and hammering and planing and sawing, or using the air compressor, the pressure washer or the vacuum. And when I was at home, it was more of the same — a wall-to-wall diet of truly dreadful rackets: more hammering, more drilling, more planing and sawing, more pressure washing. I was pretty sure he took it very personally. If there was a noise George didn't like, then I'd be making it, for sure.

I began to figure that it worked in the same way as it did with Christie: I made a noise, he made it clear he didn't like it on principle and stomped off, tail down, in a terrible huff. I swear that if he could have, he'd have put his paws over his ears. As it was, he had this irritated 'haruumph!' sound he'd make instead, which did the job almost as well.

So far, this was all pretty normal dog behaviour. When your nose and your ears are as acute as a dog's are, you tend to be sensitive about that kind of stuff. But George also hated water, which *was* odd. Dogs are supposed to like water — they are natural swimmers — and images of dogs playing in the sea are classic, as are dogs horsing around under sprinklers, fording streams, tails a-wagging, and shaking themselves dry and dousing everyone around.

But it wasn't for George. He found all water deeply unsettling and hated getting his giant paws wet, which seemed a shame, because the Arizona summer was in full, scorching swing. The Saguaro and Barrel cacti were in full bloom, the olive and mesquite trees lush as well. Finally, we could take advantage of the pool in our yard. It was one of the features that, though pretty old, actually worked. It was a real blessing, because when it's 44 degrees, and you want to be outside, you need shade and you need water — lots of it.

George didn't like this one bit. If Christie and I went in the pool, he'd start acting anxious, putting his head down low and barking pretty constantly, pacing up and down the pool rim as he did so. No dip in the water ever went unaccompanied by this very vocal expression of his disapproval at our antics; it's something that continues to this day.

To be fair, I might have had a hand in his continued terror. One day that summer I made a decision. It seemed completely crazy that our pet didn't like water. I thought *all* dogs liked water, just as all cats did not. I'd also always thought that if you put a dog in water, he'd start to swim. Wasn't that what the doggie paddle was all about?

Of course, I didn't know anything much about it. I just figured that the solution lay in letting him see how good it was. Once I'd done that, I thought, we'd be away. I was keen that he should be able to cool off in the pool with us. Arizona summers were relentlessly hot, and it seemed crazy to have our fella mincing around on the hot patio stones, in a flap, every time Christie and I wanted to take a dip.

In short, I decided that if George was *made*

to get in the pool, he'd discover his true identity as a water-loving animal, and swim like he was born to. I was determined about this. Now all I had to do was get him in, but there was no question of carrying him in. So, without telling Christie (whatever my logic, I was pretty sure she'd say no to this), I kind of nudged him in with me one morning by coming up behind him, then looping my arm tightly around his flank as I jumped in myself.

I wasn't at all prepared for the reaction to this stunt. George was as mad as mad could be. In fact, if he had had the power of speech, I'm guessing the air would have turned as blue as the Tucson sky. As it was, we must have lost a good few gallons of the pool water as he thrashed about, the whites of his eyes showing, his limbs kicking out like four pistons. Not knowing quite what to do next, and being showered with pool water, I half pushed and half steered the seething mass of legs and ears and fur, until eventually I steered him to the steps at the shallow end, where he scrambled frantically, and furiously, back out onto dry land.

Hearing the commotion, Christie, who'd been doing some tidying up inside, now appeared at the bedroom patio doors. 'What on *earth* is going on there?' she exclaimed, looking horrified.

George was shaking himself dry at an incredible rate — he looked like some sort of mad canine washing machine hopped up on caffeine. Christie looked at me now, working out where he'd been. 'He went *in* there?' she asked me incredulously.

I nodded.

'Seriously?' she asked, shaking her head. 'Who'd have thought it?'

I got out myself, then walked across and gently patted George's damp flanks. He looked seriously pissed off.

'But I don't think he liked it,' I said to Christie, who was still shaking her head.

'I can't believe he actually got into that pool willingly.'

'Me neither.'

'Incredible.' Then her eyes began to narrow. 'Dave, you didn't . . . '

'Didn't what? What, push him in? You kidding?'

At which point, I figured I'd better quit while I was ahead. Perhaps it was true: not all dogs *did* like water.

★   ★   ★

But if George's second worst place to be was by the pool, standing watch (the first, as I found out, was *in* the pool) then his favourite

71

place, bar none, was bed. But, once again, he was outgrowing his. He still just about fit on the single mattress, but only in one position. He could sleep that way or not at all — or with us, in our lovely king-sized bed.

'With us', for any length of time, was fast becoming untenable, as with George sprawled between us, like some over-indulged prince, we both spent half the night clinging on to the edges of the mattress. So, one day in early August, we took a drive to a bed store to get him something slightly bigger and more comfortable of his own. We had no real plan as to how we'd fit it in the bedroom, but worked on the basis that however much we lost in floor space, we'd at least make up in bed space, which meant sleep space, which mattered, we both agreed, a whole lot more.

'You have to be kidding me,' said Christie, as we pulled into the parking lot. 'One hundred and forty-seven? He *can't* be!'

Earlier I'd been with George to have his check-up with Doc Wallace, and had just filled her in on the staggering news he'd told me. 'He weighs one hundred and forty-seven pounds,' I said. 'Honest.'

I could see Christie shake her head out of the corner of my eye. 'But that's bigger than that other Dane we saw at the park, isn't it?'

I nodded. 'You mean Drake? Yup. He was

one forty, wasn't he?'

She nodded. 'Exactly! But he was a five-year-old dog; George is still only close to nine months old! He's going to keep growing for more than two *years* yet! Just how big is this dog of ours going to *get*?'

The truth was that George had soon closed in on Drake, size-wise, and what had seemed an impossibility a scant couple of months back was not a shock to me when Doc Wallace told me. When you see something change daily, that change is almost imperceptible, but when there's been a gap, you see it right off. I didn't need Doc Wallace to tell me the numbers when he'd weighed George — just his expression when he saw George had been enough.

It had also become evident that George was growing up fast. In the space of a few weeks he'd begun to tower over most of the other dogs in the dog park. And with the increase in height, and in maturity, had come a very visible increase in confidence. We finally decided it was time to move him out of the puppy park and let him mix with the adult dogs again. Now that he was older, he settled in well there. He was never aggressive and never tried to dominate the other dogs; it was great to see he wasn't being pushed around any more.

He also seemed to have a real intelligence about him, and had learned a new phrase he loved: 'dog park'. All I had to do now was say those two words and he'd become real excited, alternately bounding around and watching me intently, until his enthusiasm was rewarded when I got out his leash. I could barely open the truck door before he'd have scooted in.

Still, both Christie and I were silent for a few moments as we took in the enormity of his incredible growth spurt, and the realisation that he'd probably be growing *for at least two more years*. I parked the truck in a bay and switched off the engine. 'Maybe he's just a *really* fast developer,' I said. 'Maybe this is it. Maybe he's done with growing already.'

It was so ridiculous an idea that it hardly needed saying: it was like saying the moon was made of green cheese. 'Or, maybe,' said Christie, climbing out and pushing the door closed. 'He's just going to be one hell of a big dog.'

★ ★ ★

It's got to be said that most people don't run around buying queen-sized mattresses in bed stores for anything other than humans. And it's also true that when humans buy mattresses, they generally buy box springs and bed frames to go with them. But we just wanted a mattress — for our dog.

The assistant in the bed store didn't know this as yet, so when he bounded up to see if he could help us, he naturally assumed that the mattress we were currently lying on to try out was, as was usual, intended for us. And as it hadn't taken us long to choose it (it was big enough and cheap enough — job done), we got off it and I said to him, 'Fine. We'll take it.'

'Certainly, sir,' he said, looking extremely cheerful. It was obviously a slow day for bed sales that day. 'So,' he went on, noting down the details on the mattress ticket so he could go to his computer and check on stock, 'have you decided on a box spring and bed frame to go with that?'

'We don't need either, thanks,' Christie told him. 'Just the mattress.'

'Just the mattress?' He looked deflated now.

'Just the mattress,' I repeated.

He looked even more deflated. We'd held so much promise, yet here we were letting him down, big time. He tried again. 'You sure you folks don't want — '

I shook my head firmly. 'We only need the mattress. It's not for us,' I explained. 'It's for our dog.'

His eyes bulged. 'For your *dog*?'

He looked down at the mattress, then back at us, and back at the mattress again, his face a picture. 'For your *dog*?' he said again, and you could see his mind working. 'As in a dog? Dog singular?'

'As in dog singular,' confirmed Christie. 'He's a big dog. He's pretty much outgrown his single one.'

The assistant took a last look at the mattress, and us, before going off to see if he had one in stock that we could buy and take with us right away.

'From what I'm visualising, does the word 'big' even cover it?' he asked us as he left.

We exchanged a glance, then shook our heads. It probably didn't.

In the truck on the way home, George's new bed strapped carefully in back, we laughed at the idea that our 'baby' had grown, in less than a year, from a tiny ball who sat trembling in Christie's lap on the way home from the Phoenix airport to an animal so big that he now needed an entire queen-sized mattress to sleep on.

Perhaps now that George had it, we both agreed, gratefully, he wouldn't need to spend a big chunk of every night curled up in *our* bed, which was a bonus, whichever way you looked at it. First off it meant we might all get some better quality sleep now, and secondly, though we were not really thinking about it quite yet, it might give us the space to put our minds to the business of making human babies without our canine one coming between us.

But what was a natural transition as far as we were concerned was about to become a *big* concern for Georgie . . .

6

The Birds and The Bees

They say size isn't everything, and they're wrong. In some areas of life, it's all about size, and let me tell you, when one hundred and fifty pounds of dog gets a twinkle in his eye, size absolutely does matter.

Not having had experience with teenagers, except for being them ourselves (and we were both good as gold, obviously), we were kind of unprepared for the sudden change in George. Yes, we'd known it would be coming, and we'd known we'd have to deal with it, but the reality, now that our canine friend weighed nearly as much as I did, was a zillion times more challenging than we'd anticipated.

It was August 2006 when we first realised our boy had hit doggie puberty. It seemed almost like an overnight transformation in many ways — one minute he was a puppy, full of *joie de vivre* and energy, finding happiness in the simple act of grabbing hold of life; the next, he was rambunctious, moody and almost psycho. Mostly, instead of grabbing life by the lapels, he was grabbing onto legs — table legs, chair legs, human legs, he wasn't picky. Our puppy, like any archetypal spotty adolescent kid, had discovered how life came to be. In short, our gentle George had discovered his manhood.

He would hump anything — absolutely anything. And being the sort of size he was made for a wealth of possibilities. If he couldn't find anything vertical to hump, he would simply lie on the floor and hump that instead. And if he was in bed with us, which he still was whenever we let him, he would sit astride a leg — either of our legs, he didn't care which — and while away his time happily humping that. This was just fine for him — like most teenagers, he had a lot of hours to fill, and being a dog, he couldn't fill them by playing Xbox or writing poetry — but it was definitely becoming something of an issue for my wife.

Christie, being, I guess, a normal human female, had a particular passion for watching movies in which the women all wore bustles and had bosoms that routinely heaved from their corsets. These women also regularly swooned, caught their breath or got the vapours (sometimes all three at once) in the presence of any of those other period costume drama staples, brooding, magnificent and mostly taciturn men.

If she could have dressed me up as Mr Darcy in *Pride and Prejudice* — particularly as played by Colin Firth — I think she might have.

As it was, she would content herself with watching him on TV, and the place she most liked to do that was curled up in bed, late at night, with a glass of wine. It was on one such occasion — I was puttering around the house, doing jobs at the time — that it became clear that George's attachment to lower legs was becoming a little bit distracting for her.

'Dave!' she yelled. 'Honey, you just *have* to come see this!'

Naturally, being a dutiful and loving husband, I would always respond immediately to such requests from my wife.

'What's up?' I asked her as I entered the bedroom.

Christie gestured with her glass of wine, which along with the rest of her, was subject to a small but persistent tremor. George was there too — a great hairy mound sprawled right across her, oblivious to my coming in, oblivious to our conversation, oblivious to just about *everything*.

'Will you take a look at this animal!' she said, shaking her head. 'Honestly, Dave, it's like he's possessed!'

I noticed then that she seemed to have a

tear on her cheek. I gestured towards it. 'You okay, honey?'

She laughed. 'You know what?' she said, waving a hand towards the TV. 'I was just sitting here thinking how crazy this is. There's me sitting here, massive lump in my throat, trying not to cry, totally in the *zone*, and all the while this mutt — ' She slapped his rump. '*Georg-eee! Will you quit that!* This mutt has been going at it like a steam train! It's like the whole bed is in the epicentre of an earthquake or something. I'm honestly not sure if I'm watching a movie or on my very own personally tailored amusement ride!'

She reached for a tissue and dabbed at her cheek. 'Which really does kind of spoil the moment, you know?'

I looked at the TV, where the 'moment' was still in full flow — well, as much as these kinds of moments can be said to 'flow'. While George continued to loosen all the nuts in our bed frame, Mr Darcy or whoever (they all looked the same to me) was staring moodily out of the television screen, saying precisely nothing whatsoever. But then he didn't really need to say anything, did he? He just looked so brilliantly *unamused*.

It wasn't only the vibrating bed that was a problem, or George's endless attachment to straddling chair legs; George had morphed into this huge, manic, permanently excitable animal, who, given his massive size, was now potentially a hazard to smaller animals, whether he intended to be or not. His intentions may at all times have been both amicable and amorous, but he was one big old boy to have coming in your direction when his libido was active.

It made people squirm. With spectacularly bad timing, we first really became aware of this when my family were over for dinner one night. We'd just finished, and had moved into the living room, where my parents had settled down on one of the couches. George, who always liked to be right in the thick of it, had made himself comfortable on the other with Christie, sitting beside her in the way that he usually did — haunches on the couch, front paws on the floor.

I'd been into the kitchen to brew up some coffee, and when I rejoined them, the first thing I saw was his 'lipstick', as we'd recently taken to calling it, at 'full volume'. I went and sat beside my parents, where the view was even more arresting. Christie, of course, was oblivious. But if there's one thing you don't want to share with your folks, it's anything to do with *that* sort of thing. I also felt for them — they must have been mortified. George was a big dog, so it was completely unmissable. And they were respectable folks in their late sixties.

Conscious it was becoming a real conversation stopper, I stood up again. 'Hey, Georgie,' I said, 'you want a treat?'

'No, he doesn't,' Christie came back at me, as quick as you like. 'He's already pinched way too many scraps for one day.' She clamped an arm round him. 'No treats for you.'

I sat down again, and willed it to disappear, which it showed absolutely no sign of doing. I then tried doing things with my eyes to alert Christie, but she looked at me as if I was mad.

I was just about to overrule her and take him to the kitchen, when my dad said, 'You getting that dog fixed, Dave? Seems like he's only got one thing on his mind.'

'Sorry, Dad,' I said, as Christie suddenly became fully aware of the situation too.

'No worries,' my dad chuckled. 'We've all been there.'

★   ★   ★

Happily, George was closing on the nine months in age that Doc Wallace had told us was the earliest he could fix him. Less happily, though the gastropexy was obviously

83

important for his health and needed to be done, I felt like I was betraying George by secretly plotting to take away his manhood.

We had, for a short time, considered breeding George. As a pure blue, with not so much as a single hair of white on him, he was a potentially brilliant asset to the gene pool. Out of curiosity, before getting him we'd been to a dog show, which was held in the courtyard of a hotel in town. It was specifically for Great Danes, and had been put on by a local Great Dane Club, with owners travelling long distances from several neighbouring cities and states to be there and show their animals. We were surprised by the variety of fur colours of these Danes, and had marvelled at the amount of commitment and energy, not to mention organisation, that it seemed to take to show and breed dogs.

But the word 'commitment' said it all really. If you took it seriously, showing dogs was way too much work to be called a hobby, and even if you kept it simple and *made* it your hobby, you'd have no time for doing anything else, it seemed to us. As well as all the logistics of travelling long distances with your pet (something we would find out — boy, and *how* — in a couple of years), there was stuff like getting them trained, early on in life, specifically for the show ring, by having them learn to walk on your left at all times and training them to understand a multitude of commands. Start that too late and you probably never caught up.

Plus we were not really hobby people at this time in our lives. We both worked long hours because we really enjoyed our jobs, and in our down time, when we weren't up to our necks in the house remodelling, we mostly liked to chill. Christie liked music — to see bands, go to concerts — and we both liked to eat out (given the state of our kitchen, not really a luxury) and were getting to know all the restaurants around Tucson. We both loved the variety there was, living where we lived: steaks, lots of Mexican, as well as Thai, Italian and sushi. Not that we were picky anyway — basically, if someone else cooked it, we loved it.

All in all, we didn't think we had enough spare time to get involved in such a major undertaking as rearing a show dog. We didn't think we were set for breeding either, in the end. Though George was clearly an amazingly good specimen of Great Dane — that coat of his really did make him special and rare — we didn't see him as a stud. Had we got ourselves a bitch, perhaps it would have been the right thing to have a litter, but as things stood, we didn't see any great purpose — he was bought as a family pet and that was what he was. Evolution could probably manage just fine, we decided, without his genes being dropped in the pool.

Despite that, it was with a heavy heart that I took George along to Doc Wallace's surgical unit on a blisteringly hot day in late September. It is no small thing to put an animal under anaesthetic, obviously, but I hadn't been prepared for my feelings of anxiety about leaving him there that morning.

With both procedures to be performed, I knew he'd be under for a couple of hours and I also knew Christie wouldn't relax for a second till he was safely conscious once more. It was a weekday, of course, so we were both hard at work, though our minds and hearts were anything but.

I got my first text from Christie around eleven:

Hi hon. You heard anything yet?

Nope, I haven't. I texted back. *It's too early.*

You think? Text me soon as you do, okay?

You too.

What, text you? You think they'll call me, then? You gave them your number didn't you?

I think I gave them both.

But I have to switch my phone off in a minute. I have a meeting.

So they'll call me. And I'll text you. Don't

worry. He'll be fine

But shouldn't he be out by now???:-s

Not sure. You want me to ring them to see?

I think . . . no, it's okay. They'll call us when he's out, won't they?

They'll call us. Stop WORRYING. He'll be fine.

I do know that. It's just — what if he's not fine?

He'll be fine

You really think so?

YES. You want me to call them?

No. I'm being stupid, aren't I?

No, you're not. You're just being a mom, honey. Stop worrying

I am trying . . . :-s

You sure you don't want me to call them?

No. It's okay. xx

Exactly!

. . . and so on.

We were texting again at 11.30, and then at 11.45, and then at 12 . . . The big thing, I decided — what really blew me away — was how agitated I was about the whole thing myself. I felt guilty, obviously — it was me, a fellow male, who was responsible for removing his manhood, after all — but I was also stressed by the thought that something might go wrong, no matter how much I tried to reassure Christie that it wouldn't. And it wasn't just because I knew she'd be inconsolable, either.

It had been less than a year since we picked up our puppy, far less time since I'd cursed him under my breath (and out loud) for all the inconvenience and hassle he'd brought into my life. It had been even less time — a few hours — since I'd picked up his poops and muttered to myself about having to do such an unpleasant job every day. Yet, as I worked (I was ripping out some old cabinets that day — good, solid, take-your-mind-off-stuff toil), I had my ears on full alert for the sound of my phone and the call from the clinic with the news that it was over, and all was well — Georgie was okay.

The call came in a little after noon, and when I phoned Christie, which I did straight away, I could hear the relief in her voice too. George was supposed to stay overnight at the clinic, so they could keep an eye on him, but neither Christie nor I could imagine us not being with him that night. We wanted him home safe with us. It wasn't what normally happened, they told us, but as long as we were sure we could keep a close eye on him, they agreed we could come pick him up.

We met back at home, then set off together in the truck, and arrived around seven in the evening. We were so glad to see him, looking sleepy but well.

It was one hell of a thing to get him up into the truck, though. I couldn't help but wince when I thought about the location of his stitches, and how they must really, really hurt, especially when we hefted him up into his bed on the back seats, and he whimpered in obvious pain. But soon we were home and, though he was moving very slowly, we could see he still had a spark of the old George in his eyes.

Getting onto our bed was obviously beyond him, even though I'm betting it was the place in the world he most wanted to be. You could almost see him standing there, weighing up the options: should he risk attempting it or not? On the plus side, there'd be the comfort, but on the other, the pain — how much agony would he have to deal with to get up there? He hovered beside our bed for a moment, swaying slightly, looking tempted, but then lowered himself gingerly down onto his own bed.

He was up only once more — to totter outside into the yard to use the bathroom. In the end, he spent the entire night on the bedroom carpet, not even attempting to climb back onto his bed. But he slept soundly, even if we didn't.

7

Party Animal

Was it a displacement activity, or was it inevitable? Christie and I weren't sure, but, as we approached the end of George's first year, he seemed to have found something different to do instead of humping furniture. He'd calmed down, and then some, in the furniture department, but he'd replaced that activity with eating — eating, that is, as an Olympic sport.

It wasn't that he was obviously scoffing a lot more. He'd been eating an awful lot of food since we'd got him, and had never shown any sign of wanting to slow down. If we'd have let him, we knew he'd have eaten way more. But his growth spurt had become something different — not so much a spurt as a heavy-duty juggernaut. He was putting on weight in spadeloads, and it was showing.

His last weigh-in with Doc Wallace, which was done as a part of his post-op check, had seen him tip the scales at one hundred and eighty pounds. He definitely weighed more than me now — more than a whole lot of other guys, in fact — and he wasn't showing any sign of stopping.

And he'd not just grown wider; he'd grown taller as well. By now we'd learned not to leave anything edible on the kitchen counter, as any foodstuff that was placed within reach of a quick tongue-swipe would be gone long before you could open your mouth in amazement, let alone say, 'No George! Get down!' — although 'get down' was no longer the right command; he was *already* down, wasn't he? Likewise, the business of having a barbecue, previously such an undramatic, everyday pastime, had become similarly fraught with new dangers. Either he was too stupid to recognise it (which, on past evidence, was unlikely) or too sassy and too quick (*way* more likely, we figured), but a steak on the coals was like a siren to a passing sailor — you didn't dare turn your back for one minute or he'd have the meat off and away like lightning, and he'd have devoured most of it before you could tell him, 'Hey! That's *hot!*'

Nothing, basically, was off limits to our dog, so we had to have eyes in the back of our heads. Not only could he reach the counter, he could reach the *back* of the counter — unsurprisingly, since he could get his whole head in the sink. So it wasn't just a case of moving things out of his reach, but of putting everything away. It was either that or have things up so high on the walls that Christie couldn't reach them herself. Once again, we knew this because we tested it out. We were exploring new territory all the time.

And it wasn't just food that attracted George's interest; he'd also developed a passion for the sound of the doorbell. He would have made a brilliant recruit for Pavlov — it was textbook conditioning. He'd learned, as puppies do, that the doorbell meant visitors. And visitors meant new things to smell, and lots of stroking. Visitors meant fun and a whole load of attention. So when the doorbell rang, George jumped — all one hundred and eighty pounds of him — to go see what was up. And when one hundred and eighty pounds of excited dog is on a mission, very little is going to stand in his way.

He'd also bark like you'd never heard barking before: the bigger he'd grown, the louder it had become — it now sounded pretty much like a string of sonic booms, and would terrify anyone who heard it. And though this obviously didn't apply to anyone who knew him for the softie he really was, for those who didn't, it must have sounded truly awesome. Plus if he made it to the door with you (most of the time, it was *before* you), it was a mammoth job to stop him greeting any visitors into trembling submission, overwhelmed — literally — by his boundless affection and great quantities of flying Georgie-drool. We were beginning to learn that if we were expecting any callers, it made a lot of sense to keep him penned in the bedroom just before they got there, and to let him out only once the doorbell had rung, and the visitors were in the house, prepared for him.

We also had to be careful around paper. Georgie was developing a real personality, and it seemed that, if he'd been human, he'd be office bound, for sure, or, if not, he'd have a job working at *USA Today*. But it wasn't just newspaper he loved: George had a mania for any kind of paper. As with steaks and chops, nothing made from wood pulp was safe, as George's jaws were completely undiscriminating: magazines, reports, paperbacks, cardboard boxes, shopping bags, bathroom tissue, writing paper — he didn't care. Any and all of these he'd trail in long skeins about the house. But his absolute favourite to get his paws around was a roll of kitchen paper, which would send him into raptures of excitement. We pretty soon decided against the idea we'd had of putting a kitchen paper dispenser on the wall.

As well as turning paper into mush, George could also turn heads, which he did every time we went out. And nice though it was at first to have him arouse so much interest, the attention wasn't always that positive. We started noticing that the jokes were coming thick and fast: 'Is that a horse?' and 'Hey, do you have a saddle for that thing?' If we heard it once, we heard it a dozen times. And everyone, of course, thought they were being real smart, like we'd never heard any of these wisecracks before. It was getting a bit tiresome, but then it was pretty understand-able too. You took George out, and people noticed him. People stared.

Much less pleasant was the flip-side of this attention when we were out. It soon became clear that some folks were a little scared of our gentle giant, and some folks were a *lot* scared. We began noticing that some people — particularly people with children — would cross the sidewalk or the parking lot to avoid coming too close to him. This was sad to watch, because our Georgie clearly wasn't any sort of threat to anyone, but we couldn't do anything much about it. He was big and, to a lot of people, big equalled scary.

'I wonder,' I said to Christie one day, when we came home from Christmas shopping, 'how big the rest of his litter has turned out?'

'You know,' she said, piling all the bags of gifts on the kitchen counter, and kicking off her shoes with a relieved sigh, 'I was thinking the exact same thing yesterday, when I went down to the dog park with George. I saw Drake in the park and, you know, the difference in his and Georgie's size now is incredible. He seemed so big when we first saw him, d'you remember? But Georgie towers over him now — like, *already*. And Drake is what now, five? Makes you wonder, doesn't it? Perhaps our boy is part of some big genetic mutation or something.'

I recalled what the breeder in Oregon had told me. It was finally beginning to strike a chord. 'You know, we should get back in touch with her and try to find out how the rest of the litter are shaping up,' I said. 'Be interesting to know how they're doing, wouldn't it?'

'Particularly since she said he was the runt,' she pointed out. 'He may have brothers and sisters who are even bigger than he is.' She ruffled the fur around his ears. 'Imagine *that*!'

George, at this point, climbed his front paws up Christie's torso, in that way he always liked to do when we came home. I swear if he could talk he would've had something to say about his mom calling him a genetic mutation — not to mention calling him a runt, come to that. He looked about as runty as a mammoth these days. And he'd be right to be chippy, too — up on his hind legs, he was now taller than Christie by about a foot. Instead, he licked her face.

'I really don't think I *can* imagine that,' I said.

But I did like the idea of tracking down George's family, if for no other reason than simple curiosity about the genes that had made our pet so astonishingly big. So I got back in touch with the breeder from Oregon, who still had Georgie's mom as a pet. I told her how big George had grown since we'd bought him.

'One hundred and eighty pounds?' she said. There was silence for a moment. 'Wait a minute. One hundred and eighty pounds? You're sure? But he's not even a year old yet, is he?'

'This month,' I confirmed. 'He'll be one at the end of this month.'

'Wow,' she said. '*Wow*. That's one pretty big boy you've got there. His dad tipped two hundred, so he was big too, but not at a year old. He was *way* older when he hit that weight.'

I told her we'd been wondering about George's size, and we'd grown curious about what had happened to his siblings. I said we'd thought we might try to get in touch with the people who'd bought the other pups, and she told me she'd forward them my email address and phone number. It was only a day later that I got a call from a man in Phoenix who had taken one of George's sisters, Bella. He was really friendly (Great Dane owners, I was beginning to realise, almost always seemed to be) and said he'd love us to come and visit any time we were passing through town.

As we hadn't done anything for our first wedding anniversary and as we'd both been working flat out, pretty much — not to mention spending so much time up to our eyes in plaster and dustsheets and clutter and tools — when the call from the guy came, we both saw it as the perfect excuse to take off on a spur-of-the-moment anniversary road trip.

The distance from Tucson to Phoenix is a little over 120 miles by road, so this would be one big adventure for George to make, too. We took the truck, obviously, as he was way too big for the car now, putting the back seat down and making him a nice bed with plenty of soft blankets for him to lie on. We'd also packed a picnic, or, rather, Christie had. She'd made us turkey salad sandwiches, brought some sodas and some chips, and packed plenty of puppy chow and water for George. 'So now it's a proper family outing,' she'd remarked.

Bella's owner turned out a really nice guy, who was around our age, and lived in a beautiful and clearly much-loved home on the outskirts of Phoenix. It was new and sprawling and set in lush gardens full of hibiscus, bougainvillea and aloe. Maybe one day, I thought, we can have a pretty yard like this one, though it wouldn't be any time soon, I knew, given the junkyard that ours was at the moment. And it was good to see that big dogs — he had two of them — and nice homes could coexist without chaos.

It turned out that Bella's owner was as curious about George as we were about Bella, and he welcomed us all pretty warmly. Right off, you could see that George and Bella were siblings. Even though he towered over her, they were the spit of each other: the exact same pure blue coat, the same head shape and look. They sized each other up in the middle of the backyard, his one hundred eighty pounds to her modest one fifteen counting for nothing: he was a guest on her patch. You could see they both knew it, and he acted with due deference to his sister.

It took no time at all for them to say hi to each other. George did the thing he always seemed to do with new dogs now: he got close, rested his head and neck patiently on the other animal's flank, and waited for them to make the first move. As ever, we marvelled at his gentlemanly conduct; the word 'gentle' really seemed to sum him up. It wasn't long before the two of them went into full-on play mode, bounding round the backyard like they'd been together all their lives, while our kind host made us cold drinks and told us all sorts of stuff about Great Danes. It was a shame, we all agreed as we ended our short visit, that our pets didn't live a little closer to each other.

We parted with the promise that we'd be sure to keep in touch and that if we were in Phoenix we'd stop by again. Little did we know that in less than a few months, we *would* be back, but for a very different reason.

*   *   *

In the meantime, George's birthday was looming. He'd been around a whole year now, and living with us for not much less time than that. And Christie, it seemed, had plans for the celebrations. 'We're going to throw him a party,' she told me.

'A party for a dog?' I gaped at my wife.

'Honey, you have to be kidding me.'

It didn't look like it, though and, on balance, I should have expected it. Christie had, after all, only a few weeks before, dressed Georgie up to celebrate Halloween. She'd chosen him a superhero outfit, for reasons that weren't clear, complete with the whole collar and big cape thing. I had, at the time, risked a killer rebuke by commenting that George was our *dog*, not our kid. But it seemed it had fallen on deaf ears. She blinked at me as if I'd failed to understand, or was just stupid. Then she shook her head.

'No, I am *not* kidding, honey. It's his birthday, so he has to have a party.'

Despite the previous flight of canine dressing-up whimsy, my wife was, and is, a very level-headed woman, not generally prone to bouts of sentimentality. She's certainly not the sort to get crazy ideas — not if I keep her out of Nordstrom and Macy's and similar high-risk shopping environments at any rate. In one of those stores, let me tell you, she could go crazy in a *second*. But was I hearing her right? Was she seriously suggesting that we throw a birthday party for a *dog*? Sure, I loved our gentle Georgie — he was a pretty special kind of dog, but he was still a *dog* the last time I'd looked — not a superhero, and definitely not a baby.

But then I thought a bit more. Maybe she was thinking it would be an excuse to get some friends round. Maybe that was more what it was really all about. With the remodelling, we'd not been able to do that a whole lot, and I was aware of how short a time she'd been in Arizona, and how important it was that we develop friendships and put down roots in our new home. 'Okaayyyy . . . ' I answered. 'And where's this celebration taking place?'

She pulled another face that suggested I was lacking a few brain cells. 'At the dog park, of course,' she said. 'Where else would we have it?'

Christie was right. Maybe I *was* short a few brain cells. It probably *was* a stupid question. If you weren't planning to throw a house party — and she obviously wasn't — where else would you hold a birthday party for a puppy? T.G.I. Friday's? McDonald's? Of *course* it would be at the dog park. There were dogs, doggy owners and plenty of space there. But it still sounded ridiculous. 'But with *who*?'

'With the other dog owners,' she answered, quick as you like. 'Mom's going to be here for the weekend, plus my grandma and auntie, of course, but mostly I thought it would be something we could do with all the people we meet down at the park. I thought we could all, you know, get together with our dogs, and, well, have a bit of a party. Why not?'

And so, Christie not being one to make idle threats, a party in the dog park was exactly what we had.

It was all new and strange to me, this business of having dog friends because, the truth was that when the day came for us to celebrate George's birthday, we did so with a bunch of people — about a dozen of us in total — whose names we mostly didn't, and still don't know. We knew all the dog's names, of course; it would be difficult not to. We knew Drake, the Great Dane, but also Bart, the yappy little West Highland terrier; Chester, the highly strung liver-spot Dalmatian; Disney, the trimmed-to-within-an-inch-of-his-street-cred black poodle; and Super Mario, the appropriately named mile-a-minute Afghan hound. And never let it be said that Christie doesn't know how to organise a party. Despite there being no manual, as far as I know, called *Throw Your Dog The Perfect Party* (though there just might be) and despite there having been no precedent set (we'd neither of us attended a similar party down at Morris K. Udall Park, and I seriously doubted that there'd been one before George's), she organised a party that any dog would be proud of. There were special party hats for the different dogs, in all sorts of wild colours, with a variety of tassels, carefully sourced from the pet store. There were also games to play, treats to eat and, best of all, a big tray of 'pupcakes' — special dog cakes she'd tracked down, specifically formulated for canine tastes — which were gone in the blink of an eye.

We were a little anxious, it must be said, about Christie's 95-year-old grandma, mostly because she was such a big hit with all the dogs that we were seriously concerned she'd accidentally get knocked over in the crush. But apart from that, it all went really well. George, of course, was in his element. Showing an early appreciation for the advantages of his status in life (one we would come later to recognise, unequivocally, as his incredible star quality), he bounded around with his canine pals, mingling impressively, and lapped up being the centre of attention among both his doggie and non-doggie pals.

To an outsider, strolling past the dog park that November early evening, one glance through the wire-mesh fence would have said it all, really: dog lovers and owners really are special — a breed apart.

As for me — the Dave I'd been for most of my years, at any rate — I remember deciding one other thing that evening: this was the single most embarrassing thing I'd done, or been involved in, in my entire life. I ran around, threw balls and sticks, adjusted drooping doggy headgear, doled out sweet treats and pupcakes and took lots of photos, all the while wondering to myself (though I didn't mention it to Christie) what on earth people would think I was *doing*? To say I felt silly would have been like saying the Pope is Catholic.

Yet, as we began packing up after our hour or so of fun, with the low sun winking off the bright metallic hues of the party hats, I happened to glance across at my wife. Her face was a picture; there was no doubt about it. But it had a look I hadn't seen there before. I was used to her cool business head, her drive, her sense of humour; I was used to all aspects of the person she was. But here she looked different: she had an aura of contentment.

This party for George wasn't silliness at all — not at all. This birthday party was a sign.

8

The Road Less Travelled

Had we spoiled our dog, I wondered? Was that what had happened? Had we pampered him, indulged him, let him have his own way on one too many occasion? Had we created a rod for our own backs with this pet of ours? Had we inadvertently created a monster?

It was 23 December, at seven in the morning, with the sun rising, the way dusty and the road long. And George wouldn't go to the bathroom.

We'd set off, in the star-sprinkled Arizona dark, on An Adventure, which was now becoming, in the early morning sunshine, A Big Stress. We'd stopped first, still in darkness, on the outskirts of Phoenix, at a gas station. And he didn't need to go, which was fine. Since then, though, we'd also been through a couple of fast-food chain parking lots, without progress, and we were beginning to worry about the fact that neither place seemed to be providing whatever it was George required to have a pee.

Little did we expect such a hassle. This was

to be the sort of road-trip made famous by a dozen iconic movies: a long strip of glossy tarmac, the sun blazing down above us, balls of tumbleweed (duly tumbling), acres of dry scrub (though no iconic heat haze in December, of course), the dusty hard shoulder, the endless, unreachable horizon, the traditional plumes of dirt billowing up every time we stopped . . .

Except we seemed to be stopping rather more than we'd planned to. 'What's his problem?' I asked Christie, though I wasn't really asking Christie. I was speaking rhetorically, because it was my turn to take George, so she was sitting in the truck.

'What's his *problem*?' I asked again, this time louder, and *to* her.

She leaned out of the window and shook her head. 'I don't *know*. Perhaps he just doesn't need to go.'

'Honey, he *must* need to go. We've been travelling for four *hours*. And he's drunk, like, half a gallon. He *must* do.'

Bet this sort of thing never happened to Jack Kerouac when he was on the road . . .

★ ★ ★

It was Christmas and we were travelling to California.

We'd taken George to visit Christie's parents only once before, and this Christmas trip was a big one: about twenty or so family members would be either driving or flying in. It would be George's first big family occasion as well, and already he was behaving like a recalcitrant teenager, refusing to get with the programme.

Travelling to California was a big deal for George. We'd started out with that day trip to Phoenix, of course, and he'd been okay with that; on our first trip to California, it had been okay too. But back then he was smaller, and a whole lot less picky about where he'd use the bathroom — which kind of mattered. It was an eight-hour road trip from Tucson to Seal Beach, California, 500 miles of mostly desert country on Interstate 10. There wasn't much variety in the choice of places to empty your bladder.

But this time he was picky. Boy, was he picky. Whatever he'd picked up about life along the way, he'd definitely grown a lot more choosy. Just as he'd grown wary of Doc Wallace's tendency to prod him with needles, it seemed he'd also grown fussy about where he'd squat (which is how Great Danes always pee, male or female), so it was beginning to feel a lot less like an adventure and more like a growing headache — not to mention it might be the potential forerunner to a major medical emergency. We were currently miles, I figured, from the nearest veterinary hospital and I had visions of having to call 911 from the side of the freeway, yelling, 'I need an ambulance! I have a dog in urinary retention!' How much fluid could a dog take before his insides exploded? Surely it had gone in, so it *had* to come out.

Or did it? For this was yet another — perhaps our fourth — human — dog stand-off, or, rather, not so much a stand-off, as a wander off. This dog of ours wouldn't squat *anywhere*.

'How can he not need to go?' I said again. Christie leaned out of the truck. She seemed way too relaxed.

'He's not drunk *that* much,' she said. 'Besides, it's hot up in the truck. He's been panting it all off. He loses lots of fluid that way, don't forget.' She gestured to where George was padding in small circles in the dirt, stopping only to bend his neck to sniff the odd weed or to peer thoughtfully into the middle distance.

'Besides,' she went on, 'you know how he is about going in strange places. Maybe if we drive on a way — find somewhere a little different — '

'But in what *way* different? Italian tiles,

piped music, a bidet? And if he's like this now, how's he going to be at your parents'?'

'Oh, stop stressing, honey. Come on. Let's drive on for a bit.'

George definitely heard this; he gave me such a haughty look. He loped regally back to the truck.

And so we drove on. And on a bit further. And still on. Another bunch of miles. Another dusty hard shoulder. Another couple of hours. Another well-appointed place for going to the bathroom (a Mexican fast-food place, this time, for an early lunch) that seemed to tick all the right boxes: a good selection of soft grasses, nothing spiky, not too dusty or exposed. Yet, *again*, another bathroom refusal. He was getting like a highly strung showjumping stallion.

'Okay, you're right,' said Christie, this time the one out of the truck. 'You're right. He really *should* need to go now.'

Except he didn't, and we stressed pretty much constantly from that point. How was he going to manage once we got to California? More to the point, how were *we*?

Not Going To The Bathroom had never been something that had crossed my mind when contemplating the various downsides of dog ownership — never. Crashing into furniture, inadvertently knocking over small persons, costing a week's salary to feed, fighting neighbourhood cats — these were real considerations before we got him. But going to the bathroom? Dogs *love* going to the bathroom. Going to the bathroom was what dogs did best, wasn't it? Going to the bathroom, I'd always thought, was the doggie equivalent of John Travolta swaggering down that street, paint can swinging from his hand, in the opening scene of *Saturday Night Fever*. Since when did going to the bathroom become an issue for an animal? Particularly for a dog — dogs *love* peeing.

I said this to Christie. 'Beats me,' she said, and then she tutted. I think, by now, I might have been ranting.

But then, thankfully, to our immense relief, a whole six hours into the trip, he finally condescended to use the bathroom in the back lot of the Palm Springs branch of McDonald's, a little way off from the bins. It was a small patch of grass and it was a tense couple of moments. Once I saw him squat, I had to put my finger to my lips urgently so that Christie wouldn't start talking and distract him. To anyone watching, we must have looked crazy. We weren't sure what it said about his taste in stylish bathrooms, either, but God Bless America even so.

⋆ ⋆ ⋆

Christie's parents lived in a California cottage house situated on a bluff about a quarter mile from the Pacific Ocean. Seal Beach is a small, attractive city that sits between Los Angeles and Orange County. It isn't a big place; it has a population of around 25,000, around a third of which live in a big place called Leisure World, which is a gated community for senior citizens. Leisure World shares beach space with both a huge naval weapons station and the equally massive Seal Beach National Wildlife Refuge, which comprises around two-thirds of the land of the whole city — an odd mix, but they seemed to get on.

This wasn't the house that Christie had grown up in — her parents had moved further along the street when the children had grown up — but it was still very much a big family residence. It was bedecked, as were most of the other houses on the street, with all the stuff you'd expect for a Christmas in California. When the sun shines so brightly on your holiday decorations, you tend to rack up the ante by doing it fairly large. And like pretty much any other street in Southern California over the holidays, Christie's parents' street had gone the whole hog. There were numerous giant Santas, any number of reindeer, a bunch of sleighs parked on roofs and lawns — mostly piled high with heaps of pretend presents — plus lots of different types of snowfolk and a smattering of jolly elves. There were also enough strings of brightly coloured fairy lights to circumnavigate a good percentage of the planet. Though, as it was still daytime when we pulled up at Christie's parents', we'd have to wait till nightfall to get the full twinkling effect — us and, I didn't doubt, the good folk on Mars.

The whole house, by the time we arrived, was full to bursting with Christie's family. There was Christie's parents, obviously, plus her brother, Kevin and his wife, and their children, plus Christie's mom's siblings, of whom there were many: Christie's mom was one of seven — five sisters and two brothers. And to finish up, there was a whole bunch of grandparents, both Christie's mom's mom and pop and also her father's mom and his sister.

I don't think George had ever seen so many people of all ages and sizes assembled indoors at once. And like any dog with fondness for mass adoration (which is most dogs, let's face it), he just loved being there from the off. He could hardly stir without someone wanting to come up and pet him or sneak him treats to eat. He particularly loved the attention of the children, who, once they'd got over the immediate size-shock, did what all children did with a big friendly dog: they recruited him right off as part of their team, which he lapped up. He was completely in his element.

The other downside, apart from the Bathroom Anxiety, was that it was a bit of a tight fit getting the three of us into the small guest room (us on the pull-out, and him on the floor, on a bunch of blankets, beside us) without a hopeless entanglement of limbs. We also hated the fact that we had to leave him in the dark garage, all alone, when we went to church or out to eat.

Christmas Day, however, saw him rise to the occasion, perhaps a bit too much, given just how big he was now. The main action on Christmas morning took place in the living room, and considering the number of people and the size of the room, there was a very real prospect that he would not only step on some delicate and precious Christmas gift, but — more worryingly — accidentally topple over one of Christie's grandmas. Though, to be fair, she'd already survived George's party at the dog park, and was therefore pretty savvy and stayed mostly sitting safely in her seat.

But even if he didn't taken out any seniors directly, there was the constant worry of one of them accidentally being buried under the Christmas tree instead. George being George, i.e. obsessive about being in the middle of things, couldn't bear to sit still for an instant. He was also, of course, absolutely smitten with paper, and there was more here, at one time, than he'd ever seen in his life — lovely, brightly coloured, crackly, snappy, chewable paper. Forget choc drops, this was Christmas euphoria for George. Consequently, there was no chance of anybody opening a present without him wanting to be right in there, getting involved.

At first we thought the wrapping paper would be a useful distraction from all the other potential hazards; maybe we could shunt him to a corner and leave him to chew. But just as soon as we'd think he was happily occupied with one bit, there came the irresistible sound of another bit being torn up. That noise was just like the doorbell to George — it sent him wild with delight. It soon became evident that we were in a potentially disastrous situation: one flick of his tail, or one overenthusiastic bound to the source, and we would see that tree, all ten twinkling feet of the thing, come crashing down in the middle of the living room.

But California being kind, weatherwise, even at Christmas, we could spend a large part of the day out in the backyard. Christie's parents' backyard was beautiful, with a big patio and lots of flowers, but best of all, for George, it had grass. George had hardly ever seen grass: back in Tucson, it being desert, he was used to playing on gravel. So grass got a paws-up right away. He entertained everyone by running around the lawn in mad circles all afternoon, trying to pick up great chunks in his mouth. He didn't have much success, so the grass survived the onslaught — which was a relief — as did the huge avocado tree they had, which was dropping avocados on the grass all the time. He did try one — George would readily try any sort of new foodstuff — but, happily, they weren't to his liking.

'Just as well,' I think it was Christie's Uncle Terry who observed, 'or you might find your journey back to Tucson is memorable too — for the same, though entirely opposite reasons . . .'

★　★　★

The day after Christmas, the main event over, Christie and I snuck away and took George down to the dog beach for a couple of hours to give him his first experience of the sea. The weather was glorious, the sugar-fine sand sparkled underfoot, while swathes of diamonds danced and glittered on the water.

For George, this new underfoot experience was also brilliant. He seemed to love sand as much, maybe even more, than he loved grass, and I wondered what it must be like to be a dog, to feel life — all those sensations — in such a simple, joyous way. He wasn't the only Great Dane on the beach either — we met several others — as well as plenty of other breeds of dog, playing both in and out of the water, and right away George was bounding around happily, making friends. Christie, however, seemed in a more reflective mood.

'You seem quiet,' I told her, as we strolled barefoot along the beach. We'd bought swimwear and towels; the sea was just so inviting. It was something neither of us had seen in a good while — a whole year now. And it appeared that her mind was on the same thing as mine.

'I was just thinking,' she said, 'how beautiful all this is.' She stopped and looked around, casting an arm in an arc in front of her. 'There's something about the sea, isn't there? It just pulls you in. Pulls you back to it.'

I'd grown up in Tucson, so I guess I didn't get that. I didn't have that same visceral attachment to the coastline that you do if it's where you spent your childhood. But I'd gone there to college, and its allure had certainly managed to keep me where I was — for almost two decades, in fact. I nodded. 'And now you're seeing it, you're already imagining missing it when we leave, huh?'

She grinned. 'Kind of. It's just that days like these, you have to wonder why you ever wanted to leave it, you know?' She turned. 'Which doesn't mean I'm not happy living in Tucson. Not at *all*. It's just on a day like this, you think there's really nowhere nicer to be on the planet than here. You get that?'

'Course, I get that. Who wouldn't? And it's Christmas, of course. And we're on vacation . . . '

'And there's a million reasons why doing what we did was absolutely right. And you're right: we're on vacation, and we should make the most of it. Shall we go in for a swim?'

'Absolutely,' I said. 'Hey, and maybe we'll be able to persuade Georgie to, as well.'

'You are kidding me?'

'I'm not. Look at it, it's lovely in there! And look how many other dogs are in swimming. Maybe now he's seen them, he'll give it another go. It's not the same thing as the pool, after all, is it?'

She laughed out loud. 'Dave, you know, you really have to quit this. This dog of ours hates water. Period.'

'Correction. Hates our *pool*.'

'Because you pushed him in it.'

I tried my best to look indignant. 'No, I didn't!'

She laughed again. She clearly found this hilarious. 'Yeah, you did.' She put her arms around me. 'Dave, you are like a dad with a kid here, worrying that he doesn't make the first team.'

Now I *felt* indignant. 'I am *not*! Anyway, we should at least take him down and encourage him. At least that.'

'Well,' she laughed again. 'Good luck with that!'

Typically, Christie was right. We already knew how strong our dog's will was. There was no way I could coax George into the sea. Maybe he would've given it a shot — who knew? — but Christie had called that right too: since my misguided attempt to desensitise him to water, he was having none of it, no way, no how. Yes, he still remembered 'Poolgate', as we would come to not-so-fondly call it, and he definitely bore the scars. It didn't matter that the shoreline was crowded with dripping animals, that there were dogs swimming and paddling, splashing about, catching sticks. George's reaction to us stripping down to our swimming things and joining them was first one of bewilderment

— where the heck did we think we were going? — then anxiety, very voluble anxiety. 'Not in *there*!'

We'd go in, he'd start barking, an unbroken barrage of noise, till one of us got out and went and told him to quit fussing. But then, as soon as we went in again, he'd start up again too, till the whole thing became such a major embarrassment (not to mention noise pollutant) that we had to give up on the idea. Indeed, the last time Christie sloshed back to shore to try and quiet him, he actually stepped an inch into the water and got his paws wet, so determined was he to get behind her, herd her to safety and make sure she didn't mess with the wretched stuff again.

★   ★   ★

'Do you think it's contagious?' Christie asked me, apropos of nothing, about twenty winks short of the forty I'd planned on before heading back to her parents' place and a big family supper. We'd been drying off nicely in the Californian sunshine, and I could feel George's warm heavy bulk against the soles of my feet. A little light life-guarding had obviously tired him out too.

I opened one eye, squinting against the late afternoon rays. Christie was sitting up, arms clasped around her knees, looking up the beach towards the pier. I pulled myself up onto one elbow. I was still half asleep. 'Is what contagious?'

'I was just thinking. You know, there are how many kids at Mom and Dad's right now? A dozen or so, is it? Not all staying, obviously. But, you know, yesterday, for supper. You know — Kevin and Kate's two, Mary's teen-agers, Peggy and Mark's kids, Patty's . . . '

'And?'

'And I've been sitting here now, and look around you. There are kids, like, *everywhere*, aren't there?'

I swivelled my head to look. I'd been lying in a funny position and now I had a crick in my neck. I sat up properly and rubbed at it. 'And? I still don't get what you mean. Contagious?'

She flapped a hand, which woke George, though not for long. 'I'm getting to that,' she said. 'I was just thinking — '

'You already said that.'

'About right now, in our lives, and how something just occurred to me — do we ever see any children? You know, back in Tucson?'

I thought for a second. She was right. 'I guess not.'

'Exactly. We never do, do we? We don't know any children. And you don't see them

120

out because it's way too hot for them to *be* out. You know, like this, out and about, in the daytime. They can't be out in the daytime, not in the summer, or they'd fry.'

'I'm sure they *do* go out in Tucson.' I laughed. 'They're not vampire children, are they?'

'Yes, but *we* don't see them, do we?'

I shook my head. 'But that's only because we don't know any, like you said.'

'Or know anyone who has any.'

'And your point is?'

She looked down now, then turned to me and smiled. Except I couldn't read her, as she was wearing her sunglasses.

She carried on. 'And I was thinking, this trip . . . you know, sitting here, now. I was just thinking I might have, well, picked something up.'

'What, like a virus?' I knew she was fooling with me now, but so what? I was happy enough to play along.

She nodded. 'Like a virus. *Exactly.*' She smiled again, poked her finger in the sand and then stirred it. 'Or something like that. Because there has to be a reason.'

'A reason for what?'

'For all the thoughts I've been having.'

'Which are what exactly? What kind of thoughts have you been having?'

'Thoughts about all the children here.'

'Well? What about them?'

She pushed her sunglasses into her hair now, so I could see the whites of her eyes. 'I was just thinking how much I'd like one.'

9

Maybe, Baby

I looked at my wife without speaking for a second, and she looked back, clearly eager to gauge my expression. She must have been keen, because she lowered her sunglasses down her nose and peered at me over them professorially.

'A baby,' she explained, in her no-nonsense manner, presumably in case the long-winded nature of her announcement might have left me in any degree of doubt.

It hadn't — not at all. She'd had my full attention from the off.

'I mean, look at him,' she continued, poking a gentle toe against George's slumbering form. 'Look at how good he is with children. He's been amazing with the kids, hasn't he?' I nodded. He had; he was a real natural. 'That dog is just *made* to be part of a big family,' she went on, warming to her theme. 'He *loves* kids. He'd love it if we had a baby — I know it. He'd just *love* it. And he would so enjoy the company.'

I pondered this somewhat novel concept. I

thought, 'There's a thing: someone asks you the question, 'Why d'you decide to have a kid?', and your answer is: 'To keep our dog company'. Bit of a conversation stopper, that one.'

I didn't share this flippant insight with Christie, however, because, the truth was, even though this was a shot out of left field, I was already kind of warming to the idea. After all, to quote another, more regularly quoted truism, neither of us was getting any younger. Christie was thirty-four now and I had turned forty, so it wasn't like we had all the time in the world to think about it. And she was absolutely right about George.

'Hey, Georgie,' I said, nudging him fully awake now. 'What d'you think about all this? How d'you feel about your mom and pop becoming a mom and pop?'

Christie leaned in against me. 'More importantly, honey, how do *you*?'

I put my arm around her. 'You know what? I feel great about it.'

'You do?' she said. 'Really? You're sure you're not just saying that?'

I grinned at her. 'No,' I answered. 'I am definitely not just saying that. Ask me in a month, when the reality kicks in, and yes, it's true, you might get a slightly different answer, but — '

She grinned and put a finger to my lips. 'In which case, I'll make a note in my cell right away.'

'A note? About what?'

'*D'oh*, Dave! To remind me not to *ask* you.'

★ ★ ★

Once we'd made the decision, Christie didn't waste any time. She went about the business of trying for a baby with the same drive and sense of purpose as she'd approached getting George. So the new year began with a flurry of activity, and not just in the ways that might immediately spring to mind.

Getting pregnant, it seemed, involved absolute military precision. Not only did Christie want to have a baby, she wanted to have a baby right away. And Christie, though excited, wasn't at all naive. Our chats changed, over dinner, from what we might do on the weekend to all the facts about fertility at her 'advanced maternal age'. I don't know who coined the term 'advanced maternal age' or, indeed, who thought it would be a good idea to point it out to her so forcefully, but it suddenly became the number one topic of the moment. And, soon after, a new ritual became established in our house: the daily task of Christie taking her temperature and recording it on a little chart.

She'd been to the store and bought herself an ovulation predictor kit and a thermometer — the better, she explained, for us to maximise our chances. After all, she told me (she was impressively well-informed now) there was only a small window of opportunity in every cycle, and with us both being such busy people with such extremely tight schedules, it was in our interest to know when that window was coming up so we could make sure our respective work diaries were in tune.

Like any man, I guess, I viewed this sudden change in lifestyle with equal amounts of pleasure and trepidation. While it was good for all the obvious reasons, it also signalled — potentially — a much greater change; one that was as radical as it would be permanent.

Still, I did as instructed, showed willing and obeyed orders. And for all her anxieties about it taking months, if not years, by the end of February, Christie announced that she was pregnant.

Funny, isn't it, how some things can concentrate the mind? You wouldn't think there would be much difference between the business of trying for a baby and actually expecting one, yet as soon as Christie told me her news, there definitely was.

Perhaps I'd been living in cloud-cuckoo-land, but all the while we were trying it didn't seem real to me. It was just another plan, another project bubbling under the surface, like the various ambitions and ideas I had for real estate. We would have a baby 'one day' in the same sort of way as I would 'one day' create the beautiful home of our dreams, in which we could stay put and raise a family.

Suddenly, however, this 'one day' had a date, and it suddenly seemed terrifyingly close. I realised right away that I was going to have to speed up our house remodelling schedule. There was no way I could let this baby come into a home which still, in places at least, looked more like a building site. I wasn't able to experience Christie's pregnancy hormones, obviously, but from that point on I worked a double shift almost every day of the week. I gave myself very little in the way of time off; I'd work all day on my current development property and then all night fixing up our house.

Christie, too, for all her initial exhilaration, was beginning to feel anxious about *her* work. The trouble was that her job was to go out and sell; if she didn't do that, she didn't get paid. Not only that, if she wasn't there to look after her clients, there were plenty of others, both in her own firm and others, who'd be quick to exploit that and try to get those clients for themselves. We decided the best thing would be not to tell anyone about the pregnancy till she'd reached a point along the line where she had to.

★ ★ ★

This is where life can sometimes be cruelly ironic, because that point — the halfway point — was suddenly upon us, and fate, it seemed, had her own ideas about it. It was a Monday morning in mid-July, and a particularly warm day, when Christie arrived at the clinic for her twenty-week scan.

Her baby bump was just about showing now and her work wardrobe, consequently, was becoming smaller and more difficult to manage. It seemed every weekday started with a wardrobe malfunction and a bed heaped with discarded clothes. We had definitely reached the point where, if she didn't say something herself, someone else in her office would comment, for sure.

We'd actually been discussing it that Sunday evening over supper: how she needed to tell her boss that she was pregnant, along with her due date, of course, and prepare for the impact her taking time off would have. Paid leave to have a baby, in most states in the US, is not something a person can rely on. Sure, there's a basic right to a small amount of unpaid time off, but there was no way Christie could be complacent about the idea of sitting at home bonding with our new baby. She needed to work as late into the pregnancy as possible, and keep hold of her clients while she was away. She'd pretty much decided she'd give up work a week before, and get some sort of day care organised sooner rather than later, to be sure she had everything in place for the two months or so she hoped to stay at home.

Apart from that, there was no reason in the world for us to worry. We had already passed the major antenatal milestone. The amniocentesis had been done five weeks back, and, yes, we'd sure worried about that one. When you're pregnant and thirty-five, which was what she now was, you'd have to live on a desert island not to know all the stats about the risks for older mothers, the chief one being the increased likelihood of giving birth to a baby with disabilities. And thirty-five, it seemed, was the number that mattered. It was all 'after thirty-five, this . . . ' and 'after thirty-five, that . . . ', so we were naturally pretty anxious on the day of that procedure, and equally happy to get the all clear.

But that day had been over a month ago.

This was just a routine twenty-week scan — except it wasn't shaping up to be routine at all. And, God, how I wished I'd been there with her. It must have been a pretty scary business for Christie, lying on the couch that July morning. Having taken a couple of hours off and rearranged all her appointments, she expected the operator to point on the screen at a healthy baby, but then, inexplicably, that didn't happen.

The very worst bit of it all, Christie told me, was that period of heart-in-mouth waiting, of sensing something might be up, but not knowing quite what it might be; of noticing the subtle change in the ultrasound operator's manner, but not daring to interrupt her concentration; of lying there, transfixed, hardly daring to breathe; of the silence — a new and uncomfortable silence, one suddenly throbbing with apprehension, a silence broken only by the hum of the machine; of the feeling of the gel being swept back and forth over her stomach; of the realisation, as every second ticked by, that *something must be wrong with the baby.*

'I need to get the doctor in,' the operator told her finally.

10

Into Each Life . . .

I was at home working on the house, up the top of a ladder, when my cell phone rang. George was sound asleep on his bed in the next room over. I'd not long had this phone, and it was full of different functions. When I got it, I'd set it up to have a particular song play whenever Christie called. It was 'Golden' by Jill Scott, which we'd had played at our wedding. My putting it on my phone was, Christie told me, *the* most romantic thing *ever*. I was clearly getting the hang of being a husband.

I didn't hear the phone right off though, because of the whine of the drilling, but George did — he knew Christie's ringtone as well as he knew the doorbell, and was right away in the room with me, tail wagging, all excited. It was noticing George that made me tune in to the call. I put down the drill and climbed down to go answer it.

My phone was over on the other side of the room — our kitchen adjoined our living room — sitting on the kitchen worktop, lightly covered in plaster dust. I blew on it as I opened it and raised it to my ear. Right away, I knew something wasn't right. I could tell even before she said a word. It was one of those things I hadn't consciously thought about, yet had obviously processed on some level. Why would she be calling me otherwise? She'd already told me she was going to pop back after her appointment; she had an out-of-town appointment later in the afternoon, and was planning to change into her work suit when she got here, grab some lunch with me and George and then go on to the meeting.

'Honey?' she said. Her voice was so low I could hardly hear it. It also sounded tight, like she was trying to keep it contained.

'I'm right here,' I answered. 'What's up?'

'There's some sort of problem with the ultrasound scan,' she said levelly. 'Can you get down here to the clinic, d'you think?'

I felt a hole open up in the middle of my stomach — a stomach that now sat on suddenly heavy legs. They felt so weighty that I honestly felt like I couldn't move. I swallowed, and then asked the obvious question, 'What sort of problem?'

'I don't know,' she said. 'It's just that something's apparently not right with the baby.'

Another obvious question. 'What d'you

mean — something's not right? What are you talking about?'

I heard her exhale heavily. 'They're not exactly sure yet. There's something wrong with the heartbeat, I think.' She said this very slowly, as if trying to take it in. 'They have to take me to have another ultrasound,' she continued, 'on a different machine, over at the hospital.'

My legs felt even heavier beneath me. This was sounding more serious by the second. I licked my dry lips. 'The hospital?' I asked.

'Yes, because the equipment there is more advanced. So, if you could get here, you know, as soon as you can — ' She tailed off.

George, ever sensitive to changes in atmosphere, had come up and was standing to attention beside me, his head slightly cocked, looking at me intently. The top of his head, I realised, was covered in a light mist of plaster dust too. I smoothed a hand across it absently as I spoke.

'Sure, honey,' I said. 'Of course. I'll come down right away.'

I didn't know what else to do or say.

I left George in the cool of the house, filled up his water bowl and told him I wouldn't be gone too long. I then grabbed the truck keys, and headed out the door, anxiety snapping at my heels.

It was hot as hell that day, with the sky a deep, unbroken cerulean blue, and the surface of the road blurred and shimmered in front of me. The roads were pretty crowded — it was right in the middle of that lunchtime mini rush hour — and it felt just my luck that everyone else had somewhere important to be today. Except they hadn't, I knew they hadn't, but I *had*.

I crossed several busy intersections, all the time moving in frustratingly slow increments, red light by red light by red light, across town. As I drove, I kept thinking about the birth, about the plans we'd both already made for it, about the conversation we'd had on the subject only a few days back, about how we'd agreed, given the way the traffic in Tucson could be sometimes, that we'd need to plan carefully for when the big day came. Maybe we'd do a couple of dry runs of our intended route — check out detours, anticipate problems and so on. We'd make a few maps in our heads of all the other routes we could take if Christie went into labour during the rush hour.

It had been fun doing that, but now I wondered if we'd been premature, tempting fate in some way. But then I thought: why *wouldn't* we have done that? She was halfway down the line now. All was well. All was *fine*. It wasn't unreasonable to do that, was it? It wouldn't have jinxed us in some way? We'd got past that big milestone of the amniocentesis, hadn't we? I simply couldn't take it in. What could possibly be 'not quite right' with our baby?

It felt horribly ironic that it had been this very week that Christie had finally decided the time had come to make her pregnancy public at work. She'd had to. Her bump had just started to become difficult to hide, and would soon, we knew, since Christie had read a whole fistful of baby books, make the pregnancy not just difficult but impossible to keep secret. It would start growing, and growing fast — a bit like our Georgie had.

I had a picture of her then, curled up on the sofa, reading intently, occasionally lobbing a new pregnancy or baby fact across the room at me; this thing might happen, that other thing might not. X per cent of babies had this, that or the other. Eating kiwi fruit was good for you. We should be sure we had a certain baby gadget because 8 out of 10 mothers really rated it. I had, on some level, I guess, processed all these bits of wisdom, but for the life of me I couldn't bring one to mind now — just the picture of Christie, curled up, happily reading, our baby quietly growing inside her.

I made the last turn around a corner and the clinic soon loomed in my sights. 'What could be wrong?' I kept thinking. I drove through the entry gates, trying to get my frame of mind good and positive for Christie, circled round the low buildings and parked the car in the lot out back. There was a young couple getting into a car close by as I got out. She was heavily pregnant, and he was helping her ease into the passenger seat. She had her arm curled protectively around her huge pregnant belly. She looked like she could give birth at any time.

I thought of Christie, inside, with her tiny swell of tummy, of the baby that was growing inside *her*. I glanced again at the young woman and it hit me with a jolt. Yes, we'd come a long way, but we still had a long way to go, too. I clicked the car remote and jogged back to the buildings, across the parking lot. It couldn't be serious, surely. It couldn't. It just *mustn't*. I pocketed my car keys, pulled the door handle and hurried inside.

★ ★ ★

There are moments in life that always stay with you, aren't there? Happy moments; sad moments; moments of great wonder. But those moments when you know that a loved one is suffering, and there's nothing you can do, aren't they the very worst kind? The kind that punch you in the stomach. I felt like that then — as if I'd been punched in the gut.

Christie was standing on a corridor, just outside a doorway, waiting for my arrival beside a row of coloured fabric chairs that ran in a line against a wall. She had her phone clutched in one hand and her purse in the other, and she turned around at the sound of my approach.

She'd obviously been looking out for me, because as she saw me approaching, she turned and nodded at someone I couldn't see inside the room. She looked calm. But then she always looked calm in a crisis, even though — and I could tell only by the tiniest of details — she was feeling anything but.

I strode up and put my arms around her, giving her a big hug. Even though I knew it might cause a chink in her armour, there was nothing else for it. I had to.

'You okay?' I asked — just about the stupidest of questions.

She said yes, even so. 'I'm okay,' she said, nodding slightly. 'Honestly, I'm fine.'

I decided that I would leave my truck at the clinic and we'd take Christie's car, so that we could ride to the hospital together. As we got into it, both of us were unable, it seemed, to find anything to say. As I started the engine, I noticed that she sat in exactly the same way as the woman I'd seen when I'd arrived at the clinic — her arm curled and her left hand held loosely against her belly. Only now I could visualise the tiny being in there, clinging to life. It was difficult to watch, let alone know what to say.

Christie looked straight ahead, her beautiful profile held as still as a mask. I tried to think of something positive I could say, but nothing came. 'It'll be all right' just wouldn't work here.

'We'll get through this, honey,' I decided upon eventually, as I pulled out once again on to the baking stretch of road. 'We really will.' Her answering nod was so small as to be almost imperceptible — as if it needed to be small or she might crack.

★   ★   ★

There were only a few miles between the clinic and the hospital but, despite the traffic having eased a little now, everyone seemed to be taking an eternity to cross the junctions, like they were on some heat-induced go-slow.

We'd been told that the hospital would be

138

expecting us, and thankfully we were shown through without too much delay. This was the first time I'd set foot in the place, and I was struck by how busy it felt. Busy, but also something else: it felt cold. Not cold in terms of people, just oppressive as a building. Like it was a place where lots of bad things happened, and would happen. I tried to dismiss the feeling, but it sat there even so.

We were shown into a room occupied by a female technician or nurse, who rose, as we entered, from behind a computer station. She beckoned us. 'Come on in,' she said. 'Mr Nasser, why don't you take a seat here, while I get Mrs Nasser ready.'

The doctor, a specialist, walked in just behind us, and very quickly, it seemed, we were about to find out exactly what the problem was. I watched silently as Christie's belly was lubed up once more for the ultrasound, her hand clutched in mine all the time, small and hot.

The nurse stood to one side as the doctor worked the wand, the fuzzy blur of grey-white images changing constantly, all of them barely comprehensible to me. The silence, bar the hum of the machine, was deafening.

Finally, she finished. The nurse gently wiped away the lubricant from Christie's stomach. And then the news was delivered that confirmed our worst fears. This new doctor completely agreed with the diagnosis of Christie's doctor: our baby had multiple congenital abnormalities, and was very unlikely to survive.

We sat, holding hands still, as we took this in. How could it have happened? It simply didn't feel real to us. Five weeks ago, at the time of the amniocentesis, everything had been absolutely fine.

'How might this have happened?' Christie asked, voicing my own thoughts. 'What could have caused it?

The doctor spread her palms. 'There's lots we don't know about this sort of thing, Mrs Nasser,' she said frankly. 'Sometimes it's genetic; sometimes it's due to some congenital defect, or an infection, such as meningitis.' Christie nodded, and I remained silent. I couldn't think what to think about, let alone what to ask, so there seemed little else to say.

'But might,' Christie asked then, 'our baby still be okay? Is there any chance at all that it might survive?'

The doctor, once again, was gentle but frank with her. 'It's unlikely,' she said softly. 'It's *highly* unlikely.'

'So what happens now?' I asked her.

'What happens,' she said gently, 'is that we have to let nature take its course. The absolute best outcome, in terms of Christie's future chances of having a healthy baby, will be if we let nature do the work at *her* pace. It's going to be difficult and very painful for both of you, I know, but all we can do now, in the short term, is watch and wait. So what you need to do, Christie, is go home, carry on as normal, and we'll get you in here for scans every forty-eight hours.'

It sounded just horrible, and I could feel Christie stiffen beside me. 'But how long might all this — you know — go on?' she asked.

The doctor shook her head. 'I don't know. Not too long is my best guess.' She laid a hand on Christie's arm now. 'I'm so sorry.'

Christie was ashen-faced but dry-eyed during the short drive home. She looked brittle. She looked like she'd resolved that she *had* to keep things together so she could bear all she was going to have to endure over the coming days. I took my cue from her and didn't offer up pointless platitudes.

Then suddenly she spoke to me.

'I saw the notes,' she said.

'The notes?' I answered. 'You mean your hospital notes?'

She turned towards me and nodded. 'On the desk in the doctor's office. I took a look while I was waiting for the doctor to arrive. I

141

just suddenly really needed to know, you know?'

Now I understood what it was that she was talking about. We'd been offered the opportunity to find out our baby's sex when we'd had the amniocentesis done. And we'd decided we'd rather not know. We'd talked it over, at length, and agreed that we'd like it to be a surprise. We had no preference, anyway. We'd both been clear on that. Like any parents, all we wanted was a healthy child.

'And?' I said.

'Our baby's a little boy,' she answered.

She moved her hand again, and cradled him inside her all the way home.

11

. . . Some Rain Must Fall

We decided to call him Sebastian. We'd talked lots about names, and had already chosen a couple. If the baby was a girl, we might have called her Shane or Annabel, and if a boy, we had narrowed it down to Sebastian. And in the end, at the time we found out his sex, we had pretty much settled on that.

Suddenly the little bulge in Christie's belly, previously without any title other than 'our baby', became real in a way that, for me, was profound. I wasn't the pregnant one. I wasn't physically connected to him in the way Christie was. He was kicking by now, and Christie had more than once grabbed my hand and quickly placed it on her belly, so I could feel it for myself. It was an incredible sensation: kind of weird and kind of moving, all at the same time. But like many men, I knew that my connection to this baby would only really form properly when I held it in my arms. But now it was the life of my son, Sebastian, that hung in the balance. And in all probability — we'd agreed that hope was

143

now pointless — he would not see many more days.

Time is fixed, but how everyone experiences time is always relative, and those first forty-eight hours seemed endless. Too stressed and anxious to work properly, yet unable to fill the long, long hours, we wandered the rooms of our home mostly in a daze, while George, as ever completely tuned in, would wander with us, his tail down. I really didn't know what to do, what to say, how to *be* around Christie — this was completely new territory for both of us, this tragedy; neither of us had suffered the loss of loved ones yet, and I had no idea how best to support her.

We both agreed on one thing: we'd tell no one what was happening. Not because we didn't want or need support from our families, but because, right now, we didn't know what was happening ourselves, and, the truth was, we couldn't face having to have those conversations. We knew we'd have to have them soon enough anyway.

And at the end of those two days, during which I guess we were both in shock, there would come the first of what might be a whole series of scans, while we waited for nature to take its course. At the end of those two days, Christie had to take herself back to the hospital, lie on that same couch, get lubed up, take a deep breath and prepare herself to hear the worst. How long might this go on? How many times might she have to do this? Could it really continue this way for weeks? How — I couldn't stop thinking — would she be able to bear it?

And though I never voiced it, another thought wouldn't stop crossing my mind too: surely, *surely*, it would have been better all round if the news we'd had at that first scan had been final.

We spoke very little about what was happening to our baby during those two days. It was as if going there — picking over all those horrible 'why him?' and 'why us?' thoughts — would make a bad situation even worse. We just carried on, as we'd been told to, trying to act as normal as we could.

Christie, to my astonishment, had remained dry-eyed throughout the trip home from the hospital. She was dry-eyed all that evening, and dry-eyed the next day. At first I wondered if she was taking herself off to weep alone because she didn't want to let go in front of me, which kind of hurt, but I soon realised that wasn't what was happening at all. She was simply staying strong for our baby; she was desperately trying to keep things together. No matter how slim the thread of hope — no matter that, in truth, there was no thread at all — it was as if she wasn't prepared to relinquish her role as a mother. There was a part of her that wasn't going to give up on him — not yet.

Feeling useless and, to a large extent, superfluous, I could do nothing but be on hand and take my cue from George. For those two days, clearly tuned in to his mom's silent distress, he was a constant presence at Christie's side. When she sat, he sat too. When she got into bed, he climbed up there to be with her. When she stood, he stood also, and would pad alongside her to wherever she was going, maintaining a near constant vigil. I was stunned by how sensitive this dog of ours was.

On the second morning I took him to the dog park. It was real early and Christie was finally fast asleep. She'd become grey with fatigue, yet had only slept fitfully — we both had. Even so, I didn't doubt that what little sleep I did get was still way more than she did — she looked ashen, her eyes bruised and dark. But it was hardly surprising: it was pretty hard to sleep in such horrible limbo, when your life has already been shattered so comprehensively, yet you are still waiting for the very worst to happen — for your baby to die.

I decided to take George to the park on an

impulse. He needed to get out every bit as much as I did and, looking at the slender form of my wife curled beneath the sheets, I figured now would be the best time to do it. The sun was still low enough that the heat would be bearable, and I figured Christie would be more likely to sleep deeply if left alone. Now George was awake, he'd be right there, nosing round her, anxious to check she was okay. I scrawled her a quick note, left her phone on the bedside table, then silently beckoned George to come with me. Once again showing that same incredible sensitivity to atmosphere, he slipped noiselessly off the bed and followed me out. In the kitchen I grabbed water for us both — George was a water snob, and wouldn't touch the water at the dog park — and we slipped out of the house as quietly as we could, grabbing his leash as we went.

We had the place to ourselves, as I'd imagined we might at this hour; the only other owner was a woman with an energetic little puppy, who was on the far side of the small dog enclosure. As I waved hello, I wondered briefly why she might be at the park so very early, and wondered if her puppy, like George all that time ago, had spent the whole night howling and whimpering too. That put me in mind of a conversation I'd had with Christie a week or so back.

She'd been chatting to her mom in Seal Beach about babies, and had been reminded how early *she* used to get up. Her mom would sit, stupefied with sleep deprivation, while Christie, full of energy, greeted the dawn — 5 a.m. was a favourite waking-up time. And when she'd told me, we'd laughed about how we'd have to draw up a schedule — it was not a favourite time of day for either of us.

It was so sad to recall that, and I wished the thought away. All those plans we'd made were now for nothing.

George had made a slow ambling circuit of the park by now, but instead of continuing to explore, he was heading back towards me, tail uncharacteristically down. He was soon at my side, his expression intense. What exactly was going on in his mind?

'You know what?' I told him, stroking the silk of his ears. 'We've got some bad times ahead, Georgie boy.' He inclined his head very slightly and then nudged at my hand. 'And your mom is going to need you. Okay?'

I heard the clang of the gate then, and saw another owner come in. It was someone I knew well enough that he'd want to stop and chat. And why wouldn't he? That was part of why we came there. I made a big show of looking at my watch and stood to leave. George and I weren't up for making small talk — not today.

★ ★ ★

The next ultrasound was arranged for the Wednesday of that week and I had to reschedule a meeting I'd fixed up with the bank. It was Tuesday afternoon, and I was sitting at the breakfast bar of our opulent, stylish, very much family-sized new kitchen, which I'd pretty much finished the week before the scan; now the effort felt completely pointless.

I was going through some papers when Christie came in, and I mentioned that I was about to make the call to the bank manager. I wanted to double-check the time of the hospital appointment. Christie shook her head and told me no.

'I'll be fine, honey, really,' she said. 'Don't move your meeting.'

'You're kidding me. Christie, there's no way I'm not coming.'

'No,' she said. 'It's crazy. It'll take an age for you to get across town. Besides, I'll be coming straight from work, so I'll be driving myself anyway. It makes no sense for you to

149

shift everything just to come down while I have the scan.'

'You're going into work?'

She nodded. 'I have to. Actually, I think I *need* to.'

She seemed completely calm and composed about this. I, on the other hand, was open-mouthed. 'Honey,' I said, 'you really shouldn't be going into work right now. And I'm coming to the hospital, and that's that.'

She reached out a cool hand and laid it on my wrist. She had her 'I mean it, Dave' face on. 'Normal, remember? They said to carry on as normal. Normal is we go to work, you do your meeting. Normal is I go to the hospital and have my scan. I'll call you as soon as I'm done and they've . . . well.' She took her hand away and shrugged, petted George. 'Look,' she said. 'I'll call you, okay?'

'Honey, you need me with you. This could be — '

'No, I *don't*.' She said it more softly now. Gently. Like she knew she might be hurting my feelings, but with a look that was telling me she was going to do this her way.

I thought she'd change her mind. But she didn't.

★ ★ ★

When you marry late in life, there's a fairly good chance that you'll have spent a lot of years being mostly independent. And chances are — and this was true in the case of me and Christie — that you'll both be pretty used to being single and doing things by yourself. Christie was not only an experienced, educated, professional woman, she was also, very definitely, her *own* woman.

So, despite my protestations, she got up that morning and went straight for her scan (she'd at least agreed not to go to work first). It was only overnight that something else had occurred to me: maybe she meant it — she *didn't* want me there. She wasn't saying she didn't because she didn't want to fuss, but because she genuinely thought she'd manage the whole ordeal better if she did it on her own — just her and the professionals. Like when you're hurt about something, or feeling low, and sympathy's the one thing you can't handle. Either that or I figured she might be superstitious about what was going to happen at that scan. Be normal, act normal, expect the best, not the worst, and maybe the worst won't happen.

George wasn't himself that morning, any more than we were. He'd been antsy since he woke up, even more so when Christie left. And when I set off for my still-scheduled meeting, I could tell he didn't want me to leave him as well. Once again, as I would be in the days and months following, I was amazed at how tuned in to our emotions our dog was.

This time, because I'd been waiting for it for what seemed like forever, when I got the call, I heard it right off. I was in my truck, driving home with my cell phone beside me, and the song that was my ringtone suddenly filled the small space. For two seconds I could hardly bear to pick the thing up. As much as I wanted the waiting to be over, and as much as I knew that being in limbo was worse, I also knew that there was going to be no happy outcome, no good news for our family today. Either our son would be gone, or not quite gone *yet*. I trusted the doctor totally, and didn't doubt that for a moment. It was a case of 'when' not 'if' here.

There was a side street just ahead of me, so I quickly pulled in and parked, grabbing the phone from the passenger seat as I did so. The difference in Christie couldn't have been more marked from the way she'd spoken forty-eight hours earlier. Even as I lifted the cell to my ear, I could hear she was crying — crying hard.

'Honey?' she said, her voice ragged, coming in gulps through her tears. 'He's gone. Our baby has died.'

★ ★ ★

Christie was still crying when I got to the hospital to collect her, and she cried steadily all the way home. Once again, I'd figured she'd be in no state to drive, and now I really cursed myself for not insisting I drive her to the scan in the first place.

But it was done. We were home and I could pick up Christie's car from the hospital whenever we had a moment. That didn't matter. Right now we had more important things to do.

The doctor had explained that Christie needed to have labour induced, because the best way to deal with a situation like this was to go the natural route and let her body complete the process of giving birth. It was a horrible thing to contemplate, but the doctor reassured her that she would be sedated throughout the procedure.

We could have had it done locally, in Tucson, but we were both anxious that we didn't. Christie called on all sorts of doctors, particularly surgeons, through her work, so the chances were high that whoever saw her for this would already know or at least know of her. We figured it would be worth making the two-hour trip to Phoenix to get ourselves a little privacy. Fortunately, we managed to locate a doctor in Phoenix pretty easily, and a phone call confirmed that he could do it right away.

This meant that we'd have to travel up there real quick, and we'd need to find a place to stay overnight too. Though the procedure was typically done as a day-case, Christie would be in no shape to do such a big same-day round trip. This established, more calls were made from the hospital, and in a matter of minutes we were all set to go. We just had to head home, pack a bag and find a room.

'What about Georgie?' she said now, as I fired up my laptop to track down a place near the hospital in Phoenix where we could stay. She was curled on the sofa, Georgie's head in her lap, a tissue clasped in her hand, her eyes now raw and red.

'I guess I should call up my mom,' I suggested. 'I'm sure she'd be happy to come here and stay with him overnight for us.'

'Or we could take him,' she said, stroking his head over and over. 'Wouldn't it be better,' she suggested, looking up at me imploringly, 'if he came up there with us? I hate to think of leaving him behind.'

I noticed her other hand was still on her belly. It broke my heart to see it. How damned cruel could life be? 'I'm not sure — '

I began, feeling this was going to be one big complication. 'It might be difficult to find a hotel at such short notice that would be happy to take such a big d — '

'But could you *try*, at least?' She gestured, tissue in hand, towards my open laptop. 'I know it might be hard, but you never know. Could you try? Please?'

All at once I had a flash of insight. Of course she'd want him to come with us. *Of course.* And the very last thing she'd want to do would be to have to talk about everything that had happened, to *anyone*, to make arrangements, to sort out a bed for a house guest, but, crucially, to be parted from George. I started searching, determined to do this one thing. 'Of course I can, honey.' And I did.

We were on the road to Phoenix within the hour, and I was grateful I'd elected to drive Christie home in the truck, so there was a bed ready and waiting for George to lie on. I could go get the car after we returned home tomorrow. Christie looked pretty drained. She'd not had any breakfast either, and couldn't now, of course, in preparation for the anaesthetic — not that either of us felt like eating anyway.

I'd found a hotel online, eventually, not too far from the hospital, and I'd rung them to check that they definitely took dogs.

'Even big dogs?' I'd asked the lady. 'He's a Great Dane, so he *is* big.'

'Even very big dogs,' she reassured me. 'No problem whatsoever, sir. You all have a safe trip up, now. See you later!'

In a stroke of good luck, the hotel I'd managed to find was directly on the way to the hospital too, so all we had to do was check in and drop George off, before heading on to our appointment. But in a stroke of *bad* luck, the first thing I spotted when I went in to reception, was a sign — quite a large one — on the wall. '*Well-behaved dogs welcome,*' it said, cheerfully, by way of greeting. Then, underneath, in smaller writing, '*under 35 lbs.*'

My balance of luck evidently see-sawing now, I thanked God that I'd left Christie and George in the car. I'd done so in case we had to drive elsewhere to get to our room, as the main parking lot for the hotel rooms wasn't out front. I really didn't think, with the best will in the world, George could pass for 'under 35 lbs'. It didn't matter that we'd been told one thing, and here was quite another; I really didn't have the time or the energy to argue the point. I also figured, if they knew we'd be leaving him there alone temporarily (I thought we might be gone for a couple of hours or so), they wouldn't be too keen on that idea either, and certainly not when they clapped eyes on him. We'd both learned that people often thought — wrongly — that the bigger the dog, the more likelihood there was of trouble.

Having decided that we should make this a covert operation, I checked in, established where the parking lot was and, unbeknown to Christie, as I didn't want to stress her further, snuck our close-to-200-lb dog in through the back.

★ ★ ★

The long nightmare of waiting with so little hope was over in a very short time. I waited outside while the doctors did their thing, and in a little under three hours Christie was finally returned to me, limp and wobbly and still very drowsy from the anaesthetic, and needing, more than anything, to go straight back to sleep.

You'd think, wouldn't you, that the day would have been stressful enough. But when we returned from the hospital to the hotel, we were walking through the hall towards the corridor to our room, when we could hear the unmistakable full-throated boom-boom of George barking. I cringed. I also imagined that this was presumably the result of his hearing some noise or other — perhaps another guest entering or leaving — or feeling stressed because we'd left him behind.

We didn't know what had set him off, but we did know — for we could now imagine it so clearly — that his barking had probably been going on a while. Indeed, it must have been going on for long enough to attract some attention from the staff, for as we turned the corner, we could see two of them ahead of us — a man and a woman — hurrying towards the source of the racket. The man, I noticed, had a bunch of keys in his hand.

Christie was in no state to deal with any of this, and the vision of us being summarily ejected from our room was one I simply could not contemplate, much less allow. Gripping her more firmly than I had done thus far, I upped our speed sufficiently that we gained on them fast, calling out a 'Hello!' as I did so. One of the staff members — the woman — turned around when she heard me.

'That your dog making that racket?' she asked. She asked it none too cheerfully, either. Perhaps George had woken some slumbering regular guest from a nap, and she'd just been on the end of a rant.

'It is,' I said. 'And I'm *so* sorry. We just had

to step out, literally, for a few minutes, that was all.' She looked completely unimpressed at this news. 'But now we're back, and he'll quiet right down.'

I had got my room key out, and managed to manoeuvre so that it would be me and not them who would be opening the door. I then did so, by the absolute smallest margin I could, in order to squeeze inside and reassure and quieten George without the two of them seeing in. One peek at George's head, especially in relation to the floor level, and the game would definitely be up. Christie, who'd cottoned on, despite her droopy state, hung back in the hall, smiling wanly. I just about managed to keep George from being seen.

This was absolutely ridiculous, as well as infuriating — after all, we'd done absolutely nothing wrong! We'd brought our big dog to a hotel that said it took big dogs. Any other time, I'd be making my case — firmly. But this wasn't any other time, and this was not the day for stand-offs with annoyed hotel staff. 'I'm so sorry,' I repeated, keeping one hand on George's snout from behind the door, and beckoning Christie to follow me in. 'He'll be quiet now,' I promised. 'You won't hear a peep from him for the rest of the night.'

'Big bark on that animal,' observed the

woman. The man nodded.

'I know,' I said, necessity clearly being the mother of invention. 'People have remarked on it before, as it happens. Almost sounds like he's a Great Dane or something!'

At which point, I thanked them both and then firmly shut the door.

Mercifully, Christie was so out of it that she crawled into bed within minutes of getting back, and fell immediately into a deep, deep sleep. George and I settled slowly, the TV on low, once I'd run out — quick as quick — to get myself a pizza. And, after I'd taken him out back, late and very furtively, to use the bathroom, we took to our beds pretty early too: me into the other side of the creaky divan and him to his own bed, which we'd fashioned out of blankets, and which must have been really hard and uncomfortable. We'd made it up on the floor by the bed, right by Christie, and when I woke in the morning that was still where he was, her right hand gently resting on his flank.

12

From Little Acorns

Life goes on. It has to. Because all things must pass.

It was something I remember being told all my life, but now I understood it as a reality. Life held bad times and good times, and if we expected to enjoy the good times, then we must live through those bad times as well.

Though we would never forget the pain of losing Sebastian — Christie especially — as the days turned into weeks and the weeks turned into months, we gradually began to put the whole ordeal behind us, and look forward to the future with optimism and hope again.

They say something good always comes out of something bad if you look hard enough, and, in some ways, that was true. Though it felt slightly melancholic to anticipate the coming Christmas — recalling the previous Christmas and all those hopes not yet realised — we felt more like a family, even so. George had matured into such a wonderful dog, and was now such an integral part of our little unit, that we couldn't imagine him not being there. This was especially true for Christie. There was no way you could overstate how vital a part he'd played in helping her get over what had happened to our baby. It was almost as if it had made a man of him.

He was two years old now, and still he was growing. By Christmas 2007, when I took him for his check-up, he weighed in at a whopping two hundred and fourteen pounds — the same as a large adult male human. To think he'd grow any bigger was mind-boggling; he was such a huge dog already.

He was now completely comfortable in his ever-expanding skin, and had developed a really lovely personality. Though it was amazing to see such a big animal be so gentle, we figured that was the whole point, really. He was a gentle giant precisely because he had nothing to prove; he could take on the world, and he knew it. He didn't need to be aggressive, or pushy, or run around asserting his authority. In dog terms, he really was top dog.

He was also, officially, top eater and top pooper, and attending to his needs, at both ends of the spectrum, were, since I was the one who was most with him on weekdays, a big part of my daily routine. He would get through around one hundred pounds of dry dog food per month, plus the occasional treat of beef jerky and meat sticks, and if he had his way — and this is still the case today — he would happily eat double that amount.

Naturally, what came out of the other end of George came in equally impressive amounts. His poops were huge. They could weigh about four or five pounds and could easily fill a five-gallon bucket in a week. To deal with them we fashioned this great set of tools, basically a stiff rake and a snow shovel — you don't see a lot of snow in Arizona, it's true, but I managed to track one down online — and between them my tools did a pretty good job, even if people did sometimes stare. Dealing with his poops, of course, mostly fell to me, something I'd always kind of accepted would happen, but which seemed to have happened without it being discussed. The only comment Christie made, ever, on the subject was that they were man-sized, so it needed a man to pick them up. I couldn't fault her logic, so I let it go. It was okay. Just as long as he didn't get diarrhoea . . .

As well as keeping me occupied as his personal groomsman, George had found himself a hobby. After the holiday was over, on a wild new year's whim, I went out and got myself a golf cart. I didn't play golf; I didn't even have any plans to play. I'd noticed since we first moved into our neighbourhood that several of our neighbours seemed to tool around the area in golf carts, and it seemed a really neat way to get around. They weren't legal to drive out on the main streets, of course, but around our neighbourhood, which sprawled over several hundred acres on the edge of town, they were the perfect mode of transport on a blisteringly hot Arizona day.

Right away George loved my golf cart. In fact, once he'd taken possession of his place beside me, he was reluctant to give it up to anyone. He loved everything about being out and about in the golf cart with me. Unlike the truck, where he'd have to lie across the seat in back when we travelled, the golf cart had plenty of room for him to sit up front beside me. It was open on the sides and had a pretty high roof, and he'd sit in there just like he did indoors on the sofa, with his haunches on the seat and his front legs on the floor. And, being built for slow speeds, the golf cart had no windscreen either, so George was able to feel the wind on his face, and see, hear and smell everything around him.

But if January brought George the best belated Christmas present ever, February brought even better news for us. Christie had once again fallen pregnant.

This time, however, she wasn't excited at

all. How could she dare to be? How could either of us allow ourselves to be? As any parent who has ever lost a baby will tell you, not daring to hope is the order of the day once you realise you might be granted a second chance. You just can't let yourself believe you'll be that lucky.

Christie was terribly anxious about things right off the bat. She was unable to allow herself to relax for a moment, with the memories of Sebastian once again clamouring in her head. And it seemed her fear wasn't misplaced either. At only eight weeks in, her first scan revealed bad news — all was far from well with this pregnancy, too.

She had what was called a molar pregnancy, her doctor told her — one that would never develop properly into a baby. It was a kind of benign cancer that grew straight after conception in place of a normal foetus developing. It was, and is, an incredibly rare complication (only around one in a thousand or fifteen hundred pregnancies in the US are affected) and it seemed like the cruellest, most horrible piece of luck. Two such rare and unrelated complications: what were the chances of that?

Once again Christie had to go into hospital — for a D and C, this time — and it was while there that she was given the even more depressing news that it was important that we didn't try to conceive again for at least six months to be sure that all the traces of the tumour were gone, so that the same thing wouldn't happen again. We resolved to put the whole idea out of our minds. Perhaps this baby of ours just wasn't meant to be.

★ ★ ★

It's during times of great trauma that you know who your friends are, and we'd been lucky to have made some great friends in Tucson, having hooked up again with some guys I knew from my school days.

Paul and I had been mates since the second grade, when we both went to Sam Hughes Elementary School. Like all boys that age, we liked to hang out outside, and were particularly keen on riding our bikes. One of our first big joint projects was to build ourselves a ramp so that we could jump our bikes over our neighbours' garbage cans. We kept this going well into our teens. In fact, it was me who held the coveted Evel Knievel record for jumping the most cans at one time — sixteen!

We made friends with Jim at Tucson High. By now our sporting activities had become a bit more mainstream: I played football, Paul played golf and Jim played baseball. After we left high school, Paul and I rented a house together. A lot of good parties were held there . . .

Like me, Paul and Jim were now both married, and their wives, Lee and Dana, were really friendly too. Christie and I were soon welcomed into their group. George wasn't left out either: Dana had a dog too, an energetic Labrador called Boomer, who, despite being only half George's great size, became his absolute best friend right away.

We'd met up again at the Turkey Bowl the previous Thanksgiving. The Turkey Bowl is an annual neighbourhood event for Thanksgiving, held in late November, when families get together, play a football game and generally hang out. That day was the first time we all got together properly, and the first time any of our new friends had met George. It was safe to say that he made quite an impression.

Over the summer of 2008 we spent a lot of time hanging out. It was around then that we established a really fun new ritual: pretty much every Friday night we'd gather at Paul's house for an informal happy hour — a chance to relax over a few drinks and chips after a long week.

Paul lived close by, in a red brick, ranch-style house, and his backyard had a great outdoor living space, with a barbecue, TV, refrigerator and even a beer tap, which made it the perfect place to unwind.

As ever, George's size was a talking point at Paul's. They'd all spent time with him out of doors, but within the confines of a house you got a truer sense of how he filled a room — and how normal dog-rules just didn't apply to him.

We were used to George's counter-surfing antics at home, of course, and took care not to leave food out in places where he could get it. 'But that means everywhere!' Paul pointed out, one happy hour in late fall, when George had simply waltzed up and scooped a stray pretzel off the bar. 'There's, like, *no* horizontal surface in the average human household high enough to *be* out of his reach.'

Dana laughed. 'You're telling me! I thought Boomer was bad enough. It's like having toddlers marauding around the house again, only this time they're giant-sized ones.'

Paul gestured towards George, who was out cruising around the backyard with Boomer and Paul's children, Liam, Jake and Jami, oblivious that he was the topic of conversation. Again. 'I mean, I know it's a bit of a cliché, and I'm sure you're pretty tired of hearing it, but take a look at him, will you!

That dog is just bigger than a dog's got a right to be.'

'He's a Great Dane,' I said. 'A *Great* Dane. The clue is in the name here.'

'Yeah, but there's 'great' and there's 'great'. And I've seen my fair share of Great Danes. And let me tell you, that guy is not like any Great Dane I've seen. I mean, did you *ever* see a dog as big as he is before? Honestly?'

'No,' I admitted.

'And have you ever measured him?'

I shook my head as I sipped my beer. 'But we do get him weighed regularly. And, yeah, you're right. The doc says he's pretty big, even for a Dane.'

Paul gestured towards George. 'He's not just big. He's *huge*, Dave. And you say he's still growing?'

'In theory, he is — just about.'

'And even now, I'm betting you'd have to travel a *long* way to find a dog as big as he is, don't you reckon, Jim?' He sipped his beer again, then gestured to the motif on the glass. 'Hey, there's a thought,' he said, holding it up. 'You ever go and check out the stats?'

I didn't connect for a minute. 'What stats?'

He gestured to his glass again and grinned. 'You *know*. All the stats in *Guinness World Records*? See how big the biggest dog in the world is right now? I'm betting they'd have

169

one in there, wouldn't they? They have everything you could think of that could be awarded a world record, and a hell of a lot else you never would. Liam has a copy. I'll have to go find it and take a look for you.'

I laughed, suddenly realising what had prompted the name Guinness. 'You have shares in that outfit or something?' I said. Paul's favourite drink had always been Guinness. It was his staple first drink on Friday nights — and often his second and third, too. I shook my head then. 'And, no. No, I haven't ever checked that out, as it happens.'

'Well, I *will*. Be kind of interesting to see, wouldn't it?'

★ ★ ★

Interesting, yes, but not *that* interesting. Not so interesting that I rushed out to check it for myself. Yes, George was pretty big — maybe the biggest dog in Tucson — but I didn't doubt for a moment that, somewhere in the world, there'd be a dog — maybe lots of dogs — that was even bigger than he was. What were the chances of him being the biggest in the world, really? Pretty remote.

It was only in late November 2008, when I took George for his annual check-up with

Doc Wallace, that it occurred to me that, actually, maybe the odds weren't so long. Doc Wallace had seen one hell of a lot of dogs in his time, after all.

By now, I'd had to find new ways to manage our vet visits without trouble. As with water, when George really took against something, there was no way in the world he was going to change his mind. And there was also no way — and this was truer now than it had ever been — to make him do anything he didn't want to do. No way, as in *physically* no way.

And George didn't want to go to the veterinarian any more. Despite the good doc's fabled affinity with animals, which still held completely true once we were actually *in* there, George had obviously not forgotten that there'd been a time when he'd come into this place in possession of his manhood, and then come out again, soon after, less than whole. He was therefore very antsy about attending the doc's clinic, and would no longer, under any circumstances whatsoever, allow me to take him in by the front door. It was the same as with our doorbell at home, but in reverse. He'd see the entrance, stiffen up and refuse to enter. No *way*.

This problem was, naturally, kind of difficult to deal with. Trying to shift a couple

171

of hundred pounds of reluctant dog came under the category of 'not humanly possible' — not for one man on his own, anyhow. Not for nothing did the puppy manuals stress training so much. A dog this size did exactly what *he* wanted, so it was imperative that *you* were the boss.

And I was, in all the ways that really mattered in life, but he wasn't playing ball on this one. So I had to be clever and outsmart him with my brainpower. And, applying it, I worked out that if I drove round to the parking lot out back, I could take him into the clinic via the back door instead. Of course, he wasn't stupid, so this solution would continue working only as long as he didn't suffer any further indignities at the hands of the good doctor, but since I couldn't imagine anything worse than him losing his *cojones*, I figured we were good for the foreseeable future. And should something unpleasant involving knives or needles need to happen, then I'd just have to come up with a Plan C — a Plan C that might need to involve a whole bunch of heavy-lifting gear, but I decided we'd cross that bridge if and when we came to it.

In the meantime, George was in, and up on the doc's scales, and I was in for something of a shock. Not that it would be a complete shock when it came: there was the way the doc whistled after he'd led George up on the platform and the way his eyebrows shot up when he read off the number on the scale. But when he spoke, I knew exactly what I expected him to say. And he did.

'You know, Dave,' he said, as George stepped back down off the platform, 'in all my years in practice, I can honestly say I've *never* seen a Great Dane as big as George here. You see his weight?'

I hadn't. He now obligingly showed me. 'This dog now weighs in at two hundred and forty-five pounds.'

Now, that *did* take me back. 'Two hundred and forty-five pounds? But that's — '

'Huge, Dave. That's *huge*. That's, let me see, over *thirty pounds* more than when we last weighed him, in fact. That's way more than any Great Dane that I've ever heard of. One thirty to one sixty pounds is normal for a male, but *two forty-five*? Incredible. Just plain incredible. Not that we didn't see it coming, I guess.'

I shook my head, stunned. I knew he'd grown some, but by *that* much? I guess we just didn't see it so much when we saw him every day. 'But should he even still be *growing* at this age?'

Doc Wallace shook his head. 'No, he

shouldn't. But perhaps he's not now. He's three years old, right?'

I nodded. 'Just this month.'

'So, then, he's probably done. Or, at least, he *should* be. In fact, I'd say you'll want to be careful with his food intake. He looks great right now. His weight/build and height are all in proportion. He's in really good condition all round, in fact. But you'll need to be pretty careful from here on in. If he gets any heavier than he is at the moment, then it will potentially become harmful for his health.'

That I did know. We'd had that drummed into us from puppyhood. 'We're careful,' I told him. 'We *have* to be careful. If we'd let him, he'd eat way, way more than he does.'

The doc nodded. 'But he's in fine shape right now, as I said. So whatever you're doing at the moment, keep on doing it.' He ran a hand across George's glossy flank, then scratched his head. 'But what a size! In all my years . . . What a *size*!'

He was still scratching his head when George and I left his office.

★ ★ ★

'You'll never believe what I'm going to tell you,' I told Christie, minutes later, from the parking lot of Doc Wallace's clinic. It had

174

become our ritual, this, after my visits to Doc Wallace. We'd pile in the truck, then I'd call Christie and say, 'Hi', and she'd always say, 'Go on, then. How much?'

Except she didn't — not today. She said something completely different. She said, 'And you'll never believe what I'm going to tell *you* . . . '

She was pregnant again. George and I hurried home.

13

Guinness On Tap

This time we decided to tell no one — not a soul. We weren't superstitious people, so it wasn't that we thought we'd jinx things; we just didn't think we could handle the emotional strain of talking to family and friends about it if the worst happened and we lost this one too. No, we decided to keep it in our little family — just me, Christie and George. It was our big secret.

And from that point on, it felt like we were in this weird limbo, like the rest of our lives were on hold. Sure, we carried on as normal, did our jobs, met with friends. Even though Christie's sudden refusal to drink wine was put down to her being particularly tired (which she was) or having work in the morning (which she mostly did), when it hadn't stopped her before, happily no one seemed to notice.

And we had plenty of other things to occupy our minds: we had all but finished the building work part of remodelling the house, and for Christie, at least, we'd got to the fun part. Where I liked nothing better than to be wielding a drill or ripping up and ripping out stuff, for Christie, though she could knuckle down and get her hands dirty (and had done), the best bit was when you got to start making the place your own.

And I was happy to let her become our new project manager, and to defer to her on all the decisions that needed to be made about decorating, furnishing, which colour went with what — all that inexplicable cushions 'n' candles stuff. For once I was also happy — though this was strictly a temporary arrangement — to have her drag me into all those stores full of unfathomable girl-things and attempt to pass sensible judgement on various items, many of which I couldn't properly identify as having any sort of function whatsoever.

What we didn't do — didn't do at *all*, not for a moment — was make plans for our new lives as parents, or allow ourselves to look at any baby stuff. We'd go to a shopping mall and it would be like we were both wearing blinkers. We didn't even window-shop when we passed a baby store. In fact, we'd speed up and hurry past.

But, happily, the days and weeks passed, one by one, and each scan (every one an exercise in holding our breath) was completed without drama or bad news. And finally, some-how, we arrived at that momentous date — twenty weeks — and the scan, of all the scans and examinations and procedures the one that had loomed so large and heavy on our hori-zon.

As ever, we were braced for the worst, but, having done her examinations and taken all her measurements, the doctor told us that everything looked normal. And, by the way, would we like to know the sex?

We exchanged glances. Did we want to know that? Did it even matter? We'd already heard the news we'd wanted to hear: our baby was okay. I don't think either of us cared about the baby's gender right now.

But Christie raised her eyebrows at me as the nurse wiped her belly. '*Do* we?' she asked me.

I shrugged. I wasn't sure. Did I? I pondered. Maybe I did. 'I guess . . . ' I said finally. 'Why not?'

Because perhaps, in truth, we'd already had enough surprises — all of them, up to this point, pretty bad ones.

'Yes,' I said again, nodding. 'Go on, then. What are we having?'

'A girl,' the doctor told us. 'You're having a baby girl.'

We were both a little shocked by this news.

Me for the completely illogical reason that we hadn't really talked about a girl's name for this one, and Christie because this pregnancy had felt so like her first one that it had never occurred to her it *wouldn't* be a boy. She'd also privately — and she only confessed this to me later — been anxious about not feeling sicker than she did. We both knew that suffering from bad morning sickness might be grim to deal with, but it was also a sure sign that you were pregnant — and all the folklore says you have it worse if you're carrying a girl. Bang goes that theory, then.

And now, at long last, it felt properly real. We were having not a boy but a little baby girl, and, finally, we felt we could make plans for her arrival. It felt, if not quite like all our Christmases had come at once, at least like we could allow ourselves to get excited.

Right after the ultrasound, Christie started focusing on baby stuff at last. She'd been so longing to be able to share her joy with everyone. At the beginning of June, her sister-in-law organised a baby shower for all her family and friends back in California. Then her Tucson friends, keen to get involved too, organised another one for her in July.

We started decorating, creating our baby's nursery, and bought a new crib for it. We already had a beautiful dresser, handed down by Christie's grandma, so we painted that a rich dark red mahogany to match the crib. And since we knew it was a girl, we had no reason to be neutral, so we wallpapered the whole room with butterflies. That done, it was simply a question of more waiting, as the days and weeks began to stack up.

★ ★ ★

George naturally ignored almost everything about this. While we immersed ourselves in the idea of becoming parents to our new daughter, life, for him, carried on pretty much as normal. And why wouldn't it? Though interested in our various decorating antics and purchases (he particularly enjoyed chewing up the crib's giant box), he hadn't the slightest inkling of how comprehensively his life — life for all of us — was about to change. All he did know was that his mom was getting steadily bigger and, as a consequence, less inclined to be sat upon, which was just something he had to put up with.

Life in general was pretty good for George. He was particularly keen on our Friday night happy hour excursions. They were by now becoming an institution of sorts, though little did either of us realise back then that they'd have life-changing consequences for *him*.

It was mid-August by now, and we'd just returned home from the doctor's office. Christie was only a few weeks off her due date, so we were beginning to count down to the big day. Another day, another exam, another clean bill of health. We were both, I think, feeling this thing beginning to hit us. In a matter of days, after waiting such a long time, we were finally going to put our traffic avoidance plans into action, get to that hospital and, God willing, become a real Mom and Pop.

I felt full of energy. But then, I guess, I wasn't the pregnant one, was I? 'We should do something,' I said when we got home from the clinic. 'Take George to the dog park, then go out for food? What d'you fancy? Chinese? Thai? Mexican? Or maybe go for a steak?'

But Christie, who was getting to that point down the line where her gut had little room left to fully appreciate the many options, considered for a moment, and then shook her head. 'You know what? Actually, I'm pretty tired tonight, honey. Why don't you take George round to Paul's for a couple of hours, then grab a Chinese take-out for us on the way home.'

'You sure?'

She grinned, wrapping an arm around her enormous round belly. Then she laughed.

'Trust me, I'm *super*-sure. If I never have heartburn again, *ever*, it'll be too soon, and Chinese is the absolute worst. Plus this body's had quite enough exercise for one day. So I — or, rather, *we* — ' she ran her hand across her bump 'shall go have a long soak in the tub, while you boys — ' she paused to kiss George on his snout 'go off to happy hour and do all your boy-stuff.'

It was just getting dark when George and I headed round to Paul's house, the buzzsaw sound of cicadas loud in the still air. It was a warm evening, and, as we often did on balmy nights like these, we were having cocktails outside underneath the gazebo. Well, most of us were; I'm mainly a beer man, and Paul was, as usual, drinking Guinness.

'Hey,' he said, brandishing his glass, as I grabbed myself a bottle of beer from the cooler. 'Dave, I have news. Did you manage to catch that piece in the paper this week?'

I'd been miles away, watching the antics of his ten-year-old son, Liam, who was playing with George in the yard. It seemed incredible to think that in a few weeks from now I would be a father too, and have my own child — Christie and I would have our own little daughter — and that one day, God willing, she would be playing out in our own yard with Georgie.

'Oh, sorry,' I said, realising that I'd been miles away, and finally registering that he was talking. 'The paper. Of course.'

'So did you read it?'

'Let me see, now. What *did* I read? I read a piece about new trends in the real estate market. And, yes, a fascinating article about the Arizona tree frog. Either of those pieces the piece you mean?'

He put his glass down to fetch himself another beer and shook his head.

'No, I meant the *Guinness* piece,' he said, nodding again to his own glass as he brought it back over. 'There was an article about the Guinness World Records I thought you might be interested in. Wednesday, I think I saw it.'

I sipped my own beer. 'Oh, I've got you now. You mean there was a piece about the record for the world's biggest dog?'

Paul rolled his eyes. 'No, I mean the record for the biggest number of paper clips you can fit up your nose at one sitting when there's an R in the month. Of *course* I mean about the record for the dog.'

'Really?'

'Yes, and it turns out the world's tallest dog's a Great Dane too. Name of . . . ' He raised his voice a little. 'What was the dog's name, Lee?'

'Gibson,' said Dana, who'd just emerged

from the house with a bowl of freshly made popcorn. 'His name was Gibson.'

''Was' being the operative word,' added Paul. 'He just died. Of bone cancer, apparently.'

I shook my head. 'That's a shame.'

'But he held the record for four years, apparently,' said Dana.

'So how tall *was* he?'

'A little over forty-two inches,' said Paul. 'To the shoulder, that is. That's how you measure them, apparently — to this very precise point on the shoulder. You think George could top that?'

I glanced over at him. Who knew? I shrugged. 'I have absolutely no idea.'

'Lee!' called Paul. 'Honey, you got a tape measure in there?'

★ ★ ★

We didn't know if George could beat the record, of course. Not at that point. We'd got the tape and measured him, but not knowing exactly where the measurement should be taken from — a 'shoulder' not being a place with a lot of obvious precise points — all we could say with any certainly was that he seemed to be *around* that sort of height. And despite the whole idea of it being kind of fun,

184

I had other, more important things on my mind, like the fact that I was about to become a dad.

Three Friday night happy hours later, however, Dana had an update for us all. She came with a bunch of copies of something she had found online, buried in the news, while she'd been having lunch. Dana worked in PR and marketing, so she was pretty on the ball about what was happening in the media. 'They obviously move fairly fast,' she said, handing things out to us. The piece she'd given us was an Associated Press article she'd come across about a woman who was claiming that her dog was now the tallest in the world. The dog, who lived with her up in North Dakota, was a Newfoundland, who was also called Boomer, like Dana and Jim's Lab. He was a lovely looking dog, but the tallest in the world he was not — his height from floor to shoulder was just thirty-six inches.

'Thirty-six inches? Three *feet*?' I said, incredulous. 'But that's *way* less than George is to his shoulder.'

'Exactly,' said Dana, laughing. 'That's *exactly* what I thought. I mean, there's really no contest here, is there?'

'Doesn't seem to be,' I agreed.

'None at all,' Paul confirmed. 'None

whatsoever. You know, Dave, you really should look into this a bit further. Why don't you go take a look at the Guinness World Records website and see how you can make a submission. I think it's a pretty straightforward business.'

'And it would be fun, wouldn't it?' said Dana.

'Great fun,' agreed Paul.

'A project,' I agreed. 'An official happy hour project.' I raised my glass. 'Okay — let's do it. Here's to Team George!'

★ ★ ★

Christie was in bed fast asleep when George and I got in, so I poured myself a glass of wine and opened the Chinese take-out I'd grabbed on the way home. I then fired up my laptop on the kitchen counter, and read up on Gibson and this North Dakota Boomer for myself.

There wasn't much more to tell. Gibson had been a harlequin Great Dane — a beautifully marked dog, with black and white patches — and he'd lived in Grass Valley, California. Right away you could see he would have been our boy's equal in height but George definitely had him on weight. George was at least seventy pounds heavier

186

than Gibson, and you could tell he was much more massive generally.

Gibson had died of bone cancer, apparently, at around seven years of age — not old for most dogs but a pretty good age for a Great Dane. He'd have been much loved, I didn't doubt, because these dogs are so lovable; I imagined he'd be badly missed.

I then googled Boomer, the Newfoundland from North Dakota, but there was less to learn about him. Another beautiful animal, certainly, but Dana had been right: there was no contest between them; George was so obviously the much taller dog.

As if to confirm it, George, who'd come to join me in the kitchen, now placed a questing snout down onto the counter, in the hopes of charming me into donating some food. I swivelled the screen of my laptop so he could take a look for himself.

'What d'you think?' I asked. 'You've got six inches on this North Dakota Boomer, you reckon?'

In response, George swiped his tongue across the granite top, sweeping up all the rice that had fallen from my box.

14

And Baby Makes Four

Our daughter decided she wanted to come join the party right in the middle of yoga.

Christie had been attending prenatal yoga classes once a week for much of her pregnancy. She'd always enjoyed yoga and this class was specifically aimed at pregnant women. It would, apparently, help with her labour when the time came, and she thought it was kind of neat that she would tell our baby about all the things she'd been doing when she was still in Christie's womb.

Today Christie had felt funny right off the bat. She'd been doing squats early on and had felt a bit strange, and then, once she got down for the relaxation phase at the end, she'd become aware she might be leaking. Understandably, she really, really hoped no one would notice, but while she was putting her yoga pad away more fluid leaked out over the floor, so there was no way she could keep this to herself.

Naturally, Christie was mortified. You read all the time — well, it seems women do anyway — about the many embarrassing possibilities on offer for early labour, and all you want (and all you pray for) is that, when the time comes, it'll happen in such a way that you won't suffer public humiliation.

But, in that regard, it obviously wasn't Christie's lucky day. One minute she was elegantly lowering herself to the floor, the next — well, almost the next, and certainly as a result of it — she'd created a pretty big puddle on the floor. Still, as I helpfully pointed out, at least it was prenatal yoga, and not the ordinary kind, so there hadn't been any guys there.

Sorting herself out with the minimum amount of fuss, Christie explained what had happened to the instructor and reassured her that she'd be okay. She then called her OB/GYN to warn her she was coming, and then me to put our plan into action.

It was clear she intended to retake control of the situation, after having had it so abruptly snatched away before. No, she didn't need collecting from yoga, and yes, she was absolutely fine — right now, anyhow — and the easiest thing, given we were currently slap bang in the middle of the rush hour, would be for me to go home, grab the case she'd packed, which was in the hallway, drive to the hospital with it and meet her there.

★ ★ ★

While women, I'm sure, harbour all sorts of secret anxieties about the huge leap into the unknown that constitutes giving birth, men, in their turn, do their bit. Mainly, it must be said, they are real experts on the stress front. And, yup, right now I was feeling pretty damned stressed.

Like any other man, I made the trip to the hospital with my head buzzing with unspeakable scenarios. There's nothing to beat labour for full-on intensity, I'm sure, and let's be honest, the women of the world are welcome to it, thanks. But, at the same time, giving birth is pretty scary for a man too, because there's pretty much *nothing* you can do. Nothing you can do to help the process, barring just being there, and not a lot you can do to influence the outcome.

Naturally, as I drove towards the hospital, the outcome that weighed the most heavily was the worst-case scenario that I simply couldn't shake from my thoughts. What if this? What if that? What if the other suddenly happened? The list of possible complications seemed endless. I've since found out that I wasn't alone in this, of course, because I'm told almost every other man feels the way I did. But at the time all I could think of was what a *huge* thing it was, this whole business of bringing a new life into the world. We'd been taught that particular grim lesson already. There were just so many things that could go wrong here.

So when I arrived at the hospital to find Christie checked in, looking calm and not even mildly in agony, my racing brain calmed down no end. She told me what had happened at the end of her yoga class, and that she'd been examined and it was all systems go.

She'd been admitted around 6.30 in the evening, and within no time at all, she began having contractions. We were transferred to a private room, and settled down to watch TV; they'd told us it would probably be a while before things got going and she was keen to catch the latest instalment of *Project Runway*. But then they decided to press on and give her an epidural and, within minutes of having it, she began to sleep.

'You think George will be okay?' she asked me just before she drifted off. 'I mean, at some point he's going to need to pee, isn't he?'

'Don't you worry about that,' I said, immediately worrying about that.

'But what if . . . '

'Shhh,' I said. 'Stop fretting. He'll be fine.'

And he was fine when I got back to him, if a little put out at the hour. It was really late, well into the middle of the night, but it was the first time I'd felt able to leave Christie, and only then because the nurse promised that all would be well and nothing would happen while I was gone.

I let him out and you could tell he needed that pee real bad; you could literally see the expression of relief on his face. He was less thrilled, of course, when I sorted out his food and water and then headed straight off out the door without him.

'I'm sorry, buddy,' I told him, conscious of what a good job he was doing looking lonely and abandoned and making me feel like a heel, 'but your mom needs me, and if I don't get back before she wakes up, we are both going to have our heads on the block. I'll get back just as soon as I can, promise.'

He looked completely unimpressed, and not at all enthusiastic about the prospect of being abandoned again. Probably just as well, I decided, as I climbed back in my car, that he didn't know what was coming next.

★ ★ ★

Our beautiful daughter was born at 12.30 in the afternoon of 4 September 2009, and we named her Annabel Mary, after both of Christie's grandmas. It was a lovely name, and a great tribute to a wonderful woman, but it didn't come without careful negotiation. I was keen on Shayley, but Christie didn't like that. She preferred Quincy, which I liked even less — it sounded much more like a boy's name to me. So in the end we compromised — always a good thing to do at such moments — and the happiest day of our lives could begin properly, though not without a touch of anxiety.

Christie confided that even as she gave birth to our precious daughter, there was a part of her heart that was back home with Georgie, concerned for the state of his poor bladder. And not just his bladder, either: we were both well aware that the happiest day of *our* lives might feel like a pretty grim one for him. It was something we needed to keep in mind.

As Christie was staying in hospital for two nights, it was down to me to prepare him for the arrival of this new family member. I'd not been complacent about it either. I'd read up some, and I knew that there was potential for discord. Amiable, even-tempered and obedient as George was, I knew from finding out about the experiences of other dog-owners that I couldn't take his acceptance of Annabel for granted. Great Danes are well known for being emotional dogs, who form strong, lifelong, unbreakable attachments to the humans they live with and love. They are also vulnerable to all manner of stress-related ailments, as we already knew, and the last thing we wanted was for the arrival of our baby to cause any sort of upset for *any* of us.

To this end, I decided to use psychology. On the night after Annabel came into the world, I had Christie hand over her first cot blanket. I figured that, scent being so important to dogs, if I could prepare George by first introducing her smell, then at least I'd have laid a little of the groundwork.

It was late when I finally got home from the hospital, so right off I was on the back foot. He was at the door to greet me as soon as my key turned in the lock, but once it was clear that I'd failed to bring his missing mom back, his expression was a picture of bitter disappointment. Where was she? What exactly had I done with her? And where had I *been* all these hours? These and other similarly probing questions were writ plain as the nose on his disgruntled face. He then turned away and loped off down the hallway.

This clearly wasn't the time to bring out

the blanket, so I followed him into the kitchen instead. 'Hey, Georgie,' I called. 'You fancy a walk? Just the two of us? Go on out and get ourselves some fresh air?'

This did at least produce some enthusiasm from him. So much so, in fact, that I knew I was on to a winner, and, since it was such a lovely late summer evening, I decided to spoil him and get the golf cart out too.

He was so excited at this prospect that he started barking, and I could hear the thunderous noise booming through the hallway of the house as I reversed the cart out into the road. He was beside himself, I knew, by the time he heard the sound of it out front, and once I'd parked it and opened the front door, he streaked out like a rocket and jumped straight into the front, immediately moving across to the passenger seat — *his* seat. Right away he was ready to go, with his head — which was now so big it stuck out through the front space — poised to catch all the exciting evening scents.

From this regal position, he was also well placed to drip great strings of drool all over the dashboard and hood. Most days it came out, particularly in the hot summer months, saw me having to hose it off. I turned on the headlights, and soon we were cruising through the darkness and the velvety night air, passing neighbours, who were used to George now, of course, and waving hellos as we sped by.

We stayed out for a good while — twenty minutes or so — because it just felt so great to be out there. I was still taking in the enormity of everything. I was a *father*. It didn't seem quite real. But eventually I figured we'd been out long enough, and swung the cart round to head back home.

Sadly, George didn't share my enthusiasm for home and refused point-blank to get out of the cart. It took every ounce of my strength and my entire bodyweight against him to finally persuade him to come back indoors. Only then, once he'd enjoyed our spot of post-natal male bonding, did I finally produce the tiny blanket.

'Hey, Georgie,' I told him. 'This blanket is from Annabel. Annabel's our baby daughter and she's coming home real soon, and you and she are going to be the very best of friends.' Luckily there was no one around to hear me besides George.

Unsurprisingly, his reaction to this statement was minimal. The blanket, however, with its rich pot-pourri of new odours, did a better job of holding his attention — but only for five seconds or so, no more. And having completed his analysis, he turned on his heel and loped off to lie down on his bed. I went to the kitchen to make myself some dinner and call the family. Who knew if the blanket had done any good? It would be a case of wait and see.

★　★　★

To say that George was in any way distressed at Annabel's arrival would be to paint a completely misleading picture. He wasn't distressed at all; he was just completely uninterested. From the moment she arrived home he made it clear as clear could be that he wanted absolutely nothing to do with her. Yes, he sniffed her from a distance once or twice when Christie tried to coax him, but after that he ignored her completely.

But if Annabel's presence was a minor irritation in the daytime — why was mom so wrapped up and tediously unavailable all the time? — at night it became something much worse.

Night-times with a new baby are a whole new experience, both for sleep-deprived parents who are dragged from their fitful slumbers and for irritable, sleep-deprived dogs. The difference was the sleepy parents had a reason to be up, and an instinct, developed over several millennia, to care for their recently born offspring.

Dogs, on the other hand, have no such driving instincts where human babies are concerned, and *this* dog was not at all happy about the changes that had taken place in his home — and, very particularly, in his bedroom. And who could blame him? For George — used to spending his nights in blissful oblivion, in the comfort of his own queen-sized mattress at the foot of the bed that was shared by his beloved owners — Annabel's high-decibel presence simply wasn't on.

Where once it was me huffing irritably at the sound of our new puppy's incessant nocturnal whining, now the tables had definitely turned. And funniest of all was that he sounded just like me. You'd hear him wake, and then harrumph, and then turn over in annoyance, and then, once it was clear that the racket was going to continue, exhale heavily again to make his point. He'd keep this up till one or the other of us did that whole feeding thing we did with this new interloper, before grunting his way grumpily back to sleep. It was priceless — so much so that, were we not so exhausted, we'd probably have been crying with laughter.

15

The Rising of a Star

George's reaction to Annabel joining our family was showing no signs of improving. Indeed, his initial indifference and irritation turned out to be a symptom of a sulk that would endure for four long months.

Still, we reasoned, he'd get used to her in time — he had to; he didn't have a choice. In the meantime, we could live with indifference, which was far preferable to him displaying any kind of hostility towards her. Not that we ever worried on that score, because though Georgie had turned out to be a champion sulker, he didn't have a hostile bone in his body. He just carried on as if Annabel wasn't there.

But while George was practising to become Most Martyred Dog in Tucson, little did he know we had bigger ambitions for him. While Annabel slept, Christie soon got to work for our newly christened Team George, going online to complete the Guinness application, which turned out to be a lengthy and complicated business, after all. There were multiple forms that she had to fill out, plus a bunch of strict protocols to follow. You couldn't just write in and say, 'Hey, our dog's the biggest', you had to prove it, and send them the evidence. And you couldn't take a quick video on your phone, either — you had to shoot a proper movie that would provide the required evidence. You had to take measurements according to a precise set of instructions, and get along a veterinarian to oversee proceedings, plus a couple of upstanding witnesses, who'd be prepared to swear you'd done everything by the book.

It wasn't just Christie who'd been busy on George's behalf: we'd all become quite excited by the Guinness application. And though we were still seeing it mostly as a fun project, we'd started to warm to the whole record-breaking thing, and begun discussing its various possibilities. So, at the ensuing happy hours, George became the number one topic (number one, that is, after our beautiful Annabel, and my latest bunch of Besotted Dad photos).

'Can you believe this?' Paul exclaimed, a couple of Fridays later. 'I have actually managed to secure the domain name giantgeorge.com!'

Paul had worked for nearly a decade in public relations and was now in sales and marketing, so to him this was all, I figured, everyday stuff, even if it meant little to me. He had already spotted and pointed out that another record-breaking dog had his own website set up, but I'd never thought about the idea of creating one for George, let alone the relative desirability and availability of domain names. Little wonder, then, that it had never occurred to me that getting hold of the name 'Giant George' might be something that was difficult to do. I hadn't thought about it at all.

But once I did think about it, I realised it *was* quite a stroke of luck, because 'Giant George' was the sort of name that tripped off the tongue easily, like Jesse James or Big Ben or Atom Ant or Mickey Mouse. Hell, Giant George might already be a character in a cartoon for all I knew. Paul was right: once you thought about it, it was incredible that it hadn't been snapped up already.

'Amazing, isn't it?' he continued. 'So I took the plunge and grabbed it quick for the princely sum of $12 a year.'

'And you know what?' Dana added, making notes in her pad. 'We should also get on and set George up with a Facebook page too. Then we can link that — and maybe Twitter — to the website.'

Paul nodded. 'Which we'd better start

building pronto, I guess.'

I was impressed with my friends. These guys clearly knew their virtual worlds well.

'And we also need to think about getting some publicity,' Dana suggested. 'Get his name out there. Start getting some interest whipped up.'

'I've been thinking about that,' said Paul, handing out a second round of beers. 'I know this guy from back when I owned my PR agency. Name's Phil Villareal. He's a senior reporter with the *Arizona Daily Star*, and he's really good. I should get in touch and see if he wants to do the story. What d'you think?'

'Great idea,' agreed Dana.

'Great idea,' I agreed too. 'That sounds pretty damned cool. Let's do it. Hey, Georgie,' I called to George, raising my beer bottle to toast him. 'How do you fancy being famous?'

★   ★   ★

We didn't have a clue what to expect from all this, but in less than a fortnight my throwaway comment about fame had become a reality. The story about George and the big photo that accompanied it filled the whole front page of the *Arizona Daily Star* — the very paper in which I'd placed that Puppy

For Sale ad back in the spring of 2006.

The reporter, Phil, had been hooked on the story right away, and had come over to Paul's for the next happy hour to get all the background he needed. He'd brought along a photographer, who'd taken a whole load of photos for the piece. As ever, George rose enthusiastically to the occasion — you never saw a dog do such a good impression of a supermodel strutting her stuff.

And then, as they say, it all snowballed.

Dana and Paul, true to their words, had been busy. Dana had created a simple website for us to start with, with some basic facts about George, bits of news and lots of photos, as well as a guest book where visitors to the site could say hi and ask questions.

Paul, meanwhile, had set up a page for George on Facebook — a brilliant way for him to interact with his fans. While Dana managed the website, and dealt with all the emails, the page on Facebook became Paul's new baby. He'd post on it daily, updating George's status, as well as posting factoids and quotes, as if he himself was George. The kids, in particular, loved it.

With all this now in place, it was easy for folks to follow what George was up to and make contact. We knew I'd get inundated, so Paul and Dana kindly stepped in to deal with this as well, both adding their email and cell phone details so that people could easily get in touch. We also set him up on Twitter, where he gained new followers daily.

Paul's daughter, Jami, had been busy too. Along with her friend Andrew, she'd made a video of George playing at the dog park with Boomer, and they'd posted the film on YouTube. They then put links on the website and Facebook and Twitter pages, and he was amassing hits at an incredible rate.

At this point we were still only halfway through the process of trying to arrange a date with Doc Wallace for the measuring, yet it was as if George was already a Guinness record holder. Paul's and Dana's cell phones were ringing off the hook, and the emails and Facebook messages and tweets from his growing fanbase were coming in astonishing numbers.

Maybe it was a pretty slow news week — who knew? — but as soon as the paper hit the news-stands that morning of Friday 9 October it was like a publicity floodgate opened, and the story was picked up by a whole bunch of other papers, both in print and online, across the world. We also got calls from the local TV stations, wanting George to appear on their shows. We soon realised that to deal with all these enquiries individually would be a big undertaking, and had the potential to get seriously out of hand (not to mention out of paw), so Paul hit on the brilliant idea of arranging a press conference, which he suggested we could hold at the dog park.

We also realised that a press conference would be a great opportunity to distribute press packs and Giant George T-shirts, and rack up the scope of the publicity even more. So I got on the case and sourced a bunch of cheap white T-shirts and had them printed with paw prints and our website address. Paul, meanwhile, created a Giant George fact sheet, which we could hand out to people with the T-shirts.

The day itself was a huge success, and was incredibly well attended. Who'd have thought our little big dog story would attract so much interest everywhere? Yet pretty much every local print media and TV journalist turned up, many of them accompanied by photographers and vide-ographers. And it was here that we threw down our challenge: we announced that we were certain George was the tallest dog in the world, and invited all challengers to a nose-to-nose face-off. It was really good, light-hearted fun.

Once again, when the clips aired and the stories were written up, there was another great flurry of activity. And it was one such contact, close to home, that got us thinking about what a truly special dog George could be.

Paul's sister had called him because her son, Will, a second grader — just seven years old — had been telling all his school friends he knew Giant George and, as a consequence, was getting a bit of ribbing. It wasn't that bad, but he was getting seriously fed up with half the class refusing to believe him when he said he knew George. 'Yeah, right,' they were all saying, with normal childish scepticism about such claims. Yeah, he *really* knew Giant George — *not*.

Could George, Paul's sister wanted to know, maybe make a surprise visit to his school? That way not only could the doubters be silenced, but it would also be a neat thing for all the kids to get to meet George since he was such a hot topic.

Will's school, Fruchthendler Elementary School, wasn't far away — about ten minutes from our house. And as we knew George would love the chance to meet his growing band of fans, the visit — a surprise one — was duly fixed up with Will's teacher and the principal of the school.

We sneaked him in late one morning, just before recess, and had him arrive in the

206

lunchroom as the kids were filing in. The result was staggering. You never saw such an explosion of excitement. And once again, even when surrounded by a whole bunch of overenthusiastic children, George, far from getting skittish and anxious and stressed, just lapped up the attention, all the strokes and all the cuddles, as if being a superstar was in his genes.

Will, of course, was now the superstar of the class, and as for George, well, George was a hero. All animals tend to have a positive effect on kids, but the way George seemed to be able to light up a room — particularly a room full of children — really blew us away. It also made us think. We realised at that point that, whatever else happened, our gentle giant seemed to have found his calling.

But the reality of just what big national news George had become only really hit home a few days after that small local visit, when he was a story on the number one breakfast TV show in America. Watching it back, we could only shake our heads in complete wonderment. We seemed to have made a PR home run without even really trying! It was simply inexplicable. Wow.

★   ★   ★

But if George was fast becoming something of a minor celebrity, it was nothing compared to what he was about to become.

'You will not believe this,' said Dana, a couple of days later. 'I've just taken a call from the *Rachael Ray* show!'

Rachael Ray, which was made right across the continent, in New York, was quickly becoming one of the most popular national daytime talk shows in America. It was made by the Oprah Winfrey organisation and had only started in 2006 but was already a big-hitter in terms of ratings. Rachael Ray herself had been a successful chef and cookery writer; now she was one of the top TV talk show hosts too. Needless to say, then, that being asked to appear on the show was *big*. And they apparently wanted to get George on the show *now*, even though he hadn't yet won the Guinness title.

'But I told them I'd have to get back to them,' Dana added. 'Because there's the obvious problem of how we'd get him to New York.'

This was something we'd already discussed as a group. George, we were firm, was flying nowhere. Dogs were not allowed in the cabins of planes, so flying meant he'd have to travel in a hold, and it was therefore simply not an option. One thing Team George was emphatically *not* about was exploiting our beloved pet in any way. This was fun for all of us, sure, but one thing was clear: it had to be comfortable for Georgie too. No exceptions.

And *Rachael Ray* hadn't been the only invitation, but it was the icing on the cake of a number of invitations, several of which took us completely by surprise. Our phones had been ringing with requests for George that came from the East Coast of the US to Europe to Japan and beyond. We simply couldn't believe how far the story had travelled, how widely it had reached across the world. We couldn't believe some of the weird questions that were being asked about him either, like 'How big are his poops?', 'Can we get some of his sperm?', 'Could our kid ride him?', 'How fast can he eat ten pounds of sausages?' — the answer to the latter, of course, being '*Very* fast'. Our happy hours suddenly got even happier than usual, as we sifted through the legions of bizarre requests and queries. We were even approached by the Mitsubishi Car Company: could George perhaps fly out for the New York Car Show?

But George didn't need to become some nomadic jet-setting canine; he could reach out to people in the virtual world. We were happy enough to watch and marvel at his growing fanbase, and the three of us, me, Dana and Paul, would text and call daily

— several times a day — to update each other on progress.

And one item of progress towards the end of October 2009 was another brief brush with major stardom. We got a call from the people at *The Oprah Winfrey Show* — perhaps the most famous talk show in the entire developed world. They understood that George was currently in the application process for the Guinness title of tallest dog. And if so, and if he won, could we perhaps get back in touch? Because, if he did, then Oprah would really like to have him on to take part in a thread they did regularly called 'That's Incredible!'.

'Except it's not going to happen,' I said to Paul and Dana, when they told me.

'What, the *record?*' gasped Dana. 'Of *course* he'll get the record!'

I grinned and shook my head. 'Don't be daft. Not the record — George is *so* going to get that. But a road trip to Chicago is just way, way too far. Still,' I added, 'nice to have been asked.'

16

Be Careful What You Wish For

You don't get a Guinness World Record lightly. We kind of knew this, of course, because we'd already read a lot about it, and George and I had begun to put work into it.

I'd figured, early on, that the key thing that had to happen was for George to stand up to his full height. George by now had a quite astonishing vocabulary; we reckoned he probably understood around forty words. But smart as he was — and he was definitely pretty smart — it would be some trick to be able to command him to 'stand up straight!' and have him do exactly what we wanted.

No, what he needed was some good old-fashioned training, like Pavlov had done with *his* dogs. And George being George, I knew the best way to do this would be to introduce some food into the equation. I gave it some thought, and eventually came up with a plan that I thought might just work.

I began with the tailgate at the back of my truck, which was high, but not quite high enough. So I got some planks of wood — I needed four to get the level just right — and set them up on top of the tailgate. Now I had a platform that was almost, but not quite, out of reach, on which I could place treats for George to eat, as long as he stretched up as high as he could.

Once I'd settled on the plan, it was a case of George learning what it was that he had to do, and I began taking him into the garage several times a day to embark on some serious training. Naturally, he loved this new game of ours. It even got so that whenever I headed towards the garage, he'd begin to get really excited. Pavlov, I thought, would be very impressed.

I used all sorts of treats: doggie choc drops, bits of ham, lumps of sausage, but my trump card was George's favourite, grilled chicken. That's what I'd use on the day of the official measurement.

It was all great fun — for me as much as Georgie — but at the same time, the reality of our enthusiastic record-breaking campaign was one hell of a lot of work for two beginner parents with a brand new baby girl to look after. Annabel was still only a few weeks old at this stage — and the realisation of how much our lives had begun to change was only just starting to kick in. We were so new to the business of being parents to our daughter and that was a big enough job in itself.

Or, more accurately, it was a bigger job for Christie. I was somewhat swept up in the diversionary business of getting George's record application rolling in the wake of the great storm of publicity. It seemed remarkable that so much had already happened, yet we still hadn't put down our marker.

But, come late October, thanks to the kindness of friends and colleagues, we were finally ready to roll. To get George's application verified, we had a whole list of conditions. We had to have the measurement done to exact specifications, overseen by Doc Wallace — our 'qualified veterinarian' — and have it witnessed, in addition to that vital videotaping by three upstanding members of the community. In our case, these were a certified public accountant, a medical doctor and a city council member. We'd decided to make everything professional by hiring a small local film crew for the morning to make the movie that would support our application. After that, it was a case of some form filling — we needed signed notarised statements from all the witnesses and a letter from Doc Wallace, on his clinic's headed paper, confirming the accuracy of the measurement.

We all gathered in Doc Wallace's back lot,

as arranged, on 22 October 2009. George, of course, rose to the occasion with great aplomb, standing tall and statesmanlike and doing exactly what was needed, as though he knew his job here was clear: he was the world's tallest dog — he knew it, we knew it. We just had to provide the evidence.

And why wouldn't he enjoy all the fun he was having, and all these unexpected gifts of grilled chicken? While his mom was busy attending to the new, demanding creature who'd suddenly been recruited to our family, he could swan off with me — we were a bit like a pair of truants from high school, looking back — and once again be the centre of attention. It was, I guessed, like the old, pre-baby times for him, but it was now a regular occurrence, so even better.

In fact, George was beginning to develop an appointments schedule that was worthy of a Hollywood movie star with a new blockbuster to promote. And dealing with all this — from discussing with Team Giant George what to put on his website to taking him to do all his appearances — took up great chunks of my time. This supposedly little project for our happy hour nights was fast beginning to spiral out of control. I had absolutely no complaints, because I was enjoying every minute, but there was also no getting away from the fact that I was beginning to feel like George's employee.

And as much as that didn't bother me one bit, someone else was getting seriously pissed off. 'You know what?' Christie said, when I got home that evening, full of all the events of the day we'd had, and excited about making the application to Guinness. 'I'm just about done with Team Giant George stuff today, if you don't mind.'

I could see her eyes were on the bunch of things I had in my hand: the collection of paperwork, the clutch of Guinness submission forms, the newly minted video of the measuring at Doc Wallace's. And one thing her expression was definitely *not* saying was, 'Gee, honey, I'm so excited to see that! You want to run it all by me, or what?' No, her expression was actually very easily interpreted. It said, 'I am tired and I am *really* not interested in all this. I know you are, but, trust me, I am NOT.'

I put the papers down on the breakfast bar and grabbed myself a beer, and took note of the fact that she was busy greeting George with a whole lot more enthusiasm than I'd got.

'Long day, huh?' I ventured. I got flashed a quick look.

'Longer than it needed to be, for sure,' she

responded. 'You know, I've lost count of the number of phone calls I've had — at least three of them while Annabel was being fed.'

Christie was breastfeeding, so I could easily appreciate how much of a hassle this must have been for her. And when our baby wasn't feeding, she spent a lot of time sleeping — or would have, if the phone didn't keep ringing all day.

I took a mental step back. Life for Christie was tough at the moment. As for any mom with a seven-week-old baby, it was totally full-on. If she wasn't nursing Annabel, or changing her — she got through what seemed like hundreds of diapers — she was burping her, soothing her and pacing up and down. She'd walk the equivalent of miles to get her off to sleep. And once that was done, there was no rest for Christie. She still had to deal with the house and the laundry, not to mention her other 'kid', Georgie himself. She explained all this with an air of resignation, along with the fact that she'd eventually decided the best thing would be to take the phone off the hook.

'And you know what?' she went on, swilling out George's water bowl. 'I couldn't help thinking . . . '

'Thinking what?' I prompted, since she'd paused for a second. Though, looking at her body language, I was pretty sure I already knew the answer — and I was right.

'I was thinking,' she went on, 'do we really *need* all this right now?'

Not quite the answer I'd expected, to be honest. No, that was 'you're an absolute heel, Dave.' But she was on the same track, even so.

She put the bowl on the upturned crate that it sat on by the breakfast bar (his food and drink needed to be up off the floor so George wouldn't strain his neck when he ate and drank), then she straightened up. 'Think about it, Dave. Do we really need all this in our lives at this moment? I mean, I know it's all supposed to be just for fun — ' She put the 'fun' bit in visual quote marks, I noticed. 'But is it? Is it *really*? You know, it seems like there isn't a minute in the day — *every* day — when there isn't someone calling up wanting something to be organised: some interview, or appearance, or signed this and signed that. But, look — ' She spread her palms now. 'Does it even *matter*, all this? Do we really care if George is the world's tallest dog? Come to that — think about it, Dave, think hard — does *he*?'

As if by some instinct designed specifically to make a point, a little cry issued forth from our bedroom. Anxious to make myself immediately and demonstrably useful, I signalled Christie to let me go, and headed off to the bedroom, but by the time I got there, Annabel was back in sweet dreams land. I very gently replaced the covers she'd kicked off, then tiptoed out equally softly.

Back in the kitchen, George and Christie were side by side at the breakfast bar, George with his snout resting companionably on the counter, while Christie idly thumbed through the paperwork, her free hand languidly stroking his flank. Even from behind her, I could tell she was tired. She had a weary demeanour about her, and it flashed through my mind (and not for the first time) just how isolating and tiring these few weeks must have been for her. Sure, she'd had her mom come to stay with us for the first four or five days after Annabel's birth, but since then we'd been pretty much on our own.

Or, more accurately, *Christie* had been pretty much on her own, while I — and just thinking about it made me wince — had been busy having a whole heap of fun with all the excitement of setting up Team Giant George.

'Fast asleep,' I said, approaching. She turned around and smiled wanly. There were dark smudges beneath her eyes. 'Well, at least for the moment,' I added.

She replaced the sheet of paper she'd been

holding and glanced at the clock. 'Fingers crossed we'll have a half-hour to fix ourselves some dinner.'

'I'll do it. You go and, I don't know, have a soak in the tub?'

She snorted, and I was pretty sure George snorted too. Turncoat, I thought, or just pretty savvy.

'Honey,' Christie answered, 'it's not a soak in the tub that I need; it's for us to focus a bit more — and I mean all of us, as a *family* — on the things that are important in our lives at this point. It just feels like you're never here, or if you are here, you're working. Or if you're not working, you're on the phone to Paul or Dana, planning the next detail of your Giant George Total World Domination Campaign. Like I said — ' She gestured to George, who cocked his head at her. 'Does *he* care about it? No. Does any of it really matter? *No*.'

She pulled out a stool from beneath the counter and climbed onto it, then pulled the pile of Guinness stuff across to her and stabbed it. It wasn't a hard stab, but, still, it made its mark. 'I mean, look. You get this in, and it's odds-on he's going to get it. You've done enough research to be pretty clear on that, yes?' I nodded. 'And so he gets it,' she continued, 'in how long?'

I shrugged. 'A few weeks, a couple of months? I'm not exactly sure yet.'

'Right. So he gets it, whenever he gets it — say, some time after the holidays — and then he's officially the World's Tallest Dog. And everything will still be *there*, Dave — all the interest, all the journalists, all the media opportunities. Hell, who knows? He could even get an invite to the White House to do a photo shoot, maybe, with the President's new dog!'

'Hey! Great idea! I should *so* get on to that one!' I offered, attempting to match her sarcasm with a bit of levity of my own.

It didn't go down well. Christie didn't seem at *all* amused. 'That's not funny, Dave, okay? Just not funny. Look,' she said, 'I just think that right now we need to take a step back, and — no.' She paused. 'That's wrong. *You* need to take a step back, honey, *please*. And then we, as a family, can get on with the business of planning our baby's first Christmas, okay?' She looked searchingly at me, and then, eventually, she smiled. And, thankfully, it was at least one degree warmer. 'You know,' she said, 'we won't get this time back again, Dave.'

She was absolutely right about everything, obviously; one of the lessons I'd long since taken on board with regard to my wife was that in almost everything like this she was instinctively wise. 'You're right,' I agreed, nodding towards George. 'He doesn't care. And, like you say, he's not even got the record yet, has he? I guess we've all got ourselves a bit overexcited, haven't we?'

'And I'm sure I would too, in your shoes,' she said, softening. 'Pretty unremitting, this 24/7 baby care, huh?'

'I'll speak to Paul and Dana,' I went on, 'ask them to carry things for me for a while. They're loving it, and they pretty much run the website and social media stuff between them anyway. They can let everyone know that George is taking a short break. I'll just FedEx the forms in and leave it at that. Like you say, let him actually *get* the record first.'

Christie pushed the paperwork across the counter towards me, and I picked it up and squared it off neatly. If I'd had a tail, it would have been planted very firmly between my legs.

'Would a 'sorry' be an acceptable thing to offer you at this point?' I asked her sheepishly.

She grinned. 'Yup, it would. And dinner would be even better.'

17

The Dark Side of Fame

She forgave me, of course, because she could see I was sorry, but Christie had delivered a pretty clear wake-up call. Some things were so much more important than getting entries in the Guinness World Records: our growing little family, our baby, our pet, our ordinary lives.

Except something happened then that fired us up again — and this time it very much included Christie. It was early November now, and though I was aware of not letting it take over life at home, in my head I was in 'all systems go' mode.

'Right,' I said to Paul and Dana, at the next Happy Hour meeting, we've got to think about speed here. Did you see how many dogs are being entered for Guinness right now?'

Dana nodded. 'I did. I checked online yesterday. There must be half a dozen other animals lined up to try for it. If we want a shot before they go and award a new title, we are really going to have to get our skates on.'

Which we did — while George and Paul's kids played tag in the yard, we spent most of that happy hour getting everything sorted, and once it was done we racked open a bottle of champagne. Sure, we knew George was tallest, but we also knew officialdom — if we hadn't got our forms in as quickly as we did, who knew how long it would be before they decided to award the record to another dog?

But two days later, right after I'd FedEx'd the forms, a new Guinness title *was* awarded. It seemed our friendly rivalry with Boomer was already consigned to history. The title of World's Tallest Dog now apparently belonged to another Great Dane.

Not that we needed to worry — it didn't exactly change things. We'd all of us checked the stats for the other dogs who'd been entered and, by our reckoning, George was taller than all of them.

But even if that hadn't been so — if we'd somehow done the measurement wrong — we were primarily in it for the fun. This was a case of may the best man, or dog, win. What other approach was there to take about such things?

So we thought we'd make contact with the owner. We'd had great fun chatting to Boomer's owner, hadn't we? It would be great to connect and share stories about our giant pets the way owners of same-breed dogs tend to like to do. Whatever happened with the title, it was now out of our hands.

But we never did get in touch. I got a call on my cell phone, from Dana, the next day.

'You'll want to get on George's website and check out the guest book,' she told me. 'There's something really unpleasant going on.'

★　★　★

Most of us live our lives fairly peaceably. We have family and friends, and a bunch of work colleagues and acquaintances, and most of us never really have to concern ourselves with people we don't know.

But put your head above that parapet — as anyone famous would probably tell you — and suddenly, to some extent, you become public property. People who've never met you feel they have the right to pass judgement, or at the very least to comment on what you say and do.

That we'd put ourselves above the parapet wasn't in question. We'd set up a website, we had Facebook, we had Twitter, we had YouTube, and through them we connected with a whole bunch of people, ninety-nine per cent of whom were exactly like we were: dog lovers, pet owners, keen to connect and make friends.

If you're a pet owner yourself, you'll probably know this intuitively: you become part of a community of other pet owners, and like to share all the things you have in common. This happens right through from the friends we still make at our local dog park to the information that gets exchanged on all the pet-interest websites, to the forums and online communities that exist so that there are places folks can go to share anecdotes and questions about their particular breeds. Our website, plus Facebook, and Twitter, and the visits, were a part of that same human process of people enjoying connecting with like-minded souls.

But perhaps we had all been incredibly naive. Because it seemed that, despite our friendly intentions, we'd stumbled across a dark side to our Giant George project, whose existence had never once crossed our minds.

★   ★   ★

One of the most popular and useful features of George's website was the guest book where people could write comments and questions to George. It had been popular right off the bat. George (or, rather, one of us) would post something up there and folks visiting the site would read about it and comment. At any one time, there were plenty of visitors, and all sorts of lively dog-related conversations would go on. It was one of the fun parts of having the website: seeing this fast-growing global community of dog lovers coming together through becoming fans of George.

But there now, for all to see, were these really spiteful comments, saying not-so-nice things about me, the Giant George Team and, most unkindly, we thought, about George himself. These comments questioned his height and weight, and said he couldn't possibly be that tall or big. In short, they said we, and he, were frauds, and that we were exploiting George for the publicity.

To say we were aghast would be to put it mildly. Why would anyone in their right mind want to do that? I simply couldn't believe (and neither could Paul or Dana) that someone would have such a vested interest that they would go to these ridiculous lengths to trash my beloved dog. Going for the Guinness record was supposed to be fun, wasn't it? But this whole thing was suddenly making it anything but. What would cause a person to behave this way? You hear stories about such people, of course, but to witness it first-hand was a reality check. Were there really people who were so bitter and mean-spirited that they would publicly belittle another person — another family — in this way? But it was a public forum — that was the whole point of the guest book — so what could we do?

We kept a close eye on it and tried to find out what was happening; with comments beginning to appear across all our social media, we started building a picture and getting clues. The final giveaway was a post that we found on a blog — a full two-page rant — almost all of it labelling George a fraud. Now the whole unpleasant business fell into place: the blog belonged to one of the people whose dog was vying for the same Guinness record that we'd submitted George for.

We decided that perhaps this was just a one-off, that they'd been having a particularly bad day and decided to take it out on their perceived Guinness 'rivals'. It wouldn't have been the first time that sort of thing had happened, and the anonymity of the virtual world makes unpleasantness so easy. Perhaps the best thing would be to give them the benefit of the doubt, trusting that they'd realise they'd made a bit of a fool of themselves, and perhaps, having done so, they'd go away.

Within days we realised that this person was intent on some sort of mission. More comments began popping up everywhere. There was one on our YouTube video of George playing with Boomer, and several more in the comments boxes beneath newspaper articles that had been published online as well.

There was obviously nothing we could do about the latter, but one thing we could do was close the guest book on the Giant George website. It was such a shame, because we'd met all sorts of great people from around the world there, but we were also very conscious that many of George's most devoted fans were children. The last thing they needed was to log on and witness some adult, but very childish, mudslinging.

On a personal level, we felt under attack too. Particularly Christie, who, just like every other dog 'mom', was enraged that there was someone out there dissing her cherished pet. Suddenly, our 'bit of fun' — so recently the cause of some spirited marital debates about priorities — had become something quite different: a priority in itself. Now it felt like George getting hold of that title was no longer something we did for a laugh, but something we *needed* to do, we all agreed, to silence this person who was so intent on bad-mouthing us.

I was also angry. What right did anyone have to talk to people they didn't know in such an unpleasant way? Christie and I were now united. We must refocus our efforts to get that Guinness World Record and put an end to all the spiteful allegations.

The next day, therefore, I telephoned the people at Guinness to let them know that we had recently sent in our package, and we'd be grateful if George could be considered for the title. There was nothing else we could do now but wait.

★　★　★

We then tried to put the whole record-breaking business right out of our minds, and mostly we succeeded. Paul and Dana, as promised, took over the website and Facebook, while Christie and I took some time out to immerse ourselves in family. After all, that was what was most important to both of us, and the *only* thing, really, that was important to George. It didn't mean a jot to him how big or small he was. He was much more concerned with the really pressing stuff of life, like finding new ways to sneak bits of our dinners off our plates, or discovering how to wheedle an extra dog treat out of visitors.

He'd also found a new thing to enjoy after Annabel was born. Even if he didn't care for her, he loved her dolls. Being a girl, she'd already amassed around half a dozen, mostly rag dolls and cloth dolls, which she was still too young to play with, so they sat in a smiling row close to her cot. Right away, George took a shine to one of them in particular, a green stuffed doll that played a nursery rhyme when it was squeezed. George loved this doll right from the minute he saw it, and any time he got a chance he would take it off somewhere, and place it between his two front paws so it played him the tune. It was almost as if it was some kind of security blanket. We'd often find him dozing with it nestled between his paws.

And we weren't about to stop him — okay, so it was a present, but we figured we could get another one for Annabel easily enough. It was a period of such big adjustment, for him as well as us, that if it made him happy, then it was just fine by us.

And our patience was finally rewarded, come the holidays, by a softening in George's attitude towards Annabel herself. He celebrated Christmas morning by, for the very first time, not only acknowledging her presence in our lives, but also licking her hand. Bingo! We'd knew we'd cracked it at last.

If initially it felt like George had made the decision to like her, as the days passed, it became so much more than that. We felt we could see his mind working; not only had she now been accepted into our 'pack', it seemed he also understood that she was the pack's youngest member, and so was in need of, and due, our boy's affection and protection. We couldn't have had a better Christmas present.

And the new year brought good news as well. I took a call from Paul directly after the holidays were over. 'Guess what?' he announced. 'This ball is still rolling. We just hit one thousand fans on Facebook!'

I knew Paul and Dana had been doing great work, keeping both the website and social media sites fresh and active. They'd both post any news about what George had been up to, as well as photos and videos and interesting links. They trawled the Internet for interesting dog-related facts and had latterly been posting George's thought for the day — most often great quotes from inspirational figures, and links to things and places and sentiments that mattered.

No sooner had these updates been posted, Paul told me, than they'd find them commented on by a hundred plus people, from across the globe. But a thousand fans? It seemed pretty incredible. 'And growing daily,'

Paul added, 'as are the followers on Twitter. Plus we are now up to 75,000 hits on our video with Boomer on YouTube.'

No, George didn't hold any world records yet, but if it was popularity they were measuring, rather than inches, he'd have been a winner by a mile. The bottom line was that George was a very special dog, and not just in terms of his stature. If my childhood dog, Apollo, could wow the crowds with his mad antics, George seemed to wow everyone just by being George. No, he didn't goof around, or perform tricks — he didn't need to. Just being in his presence seemed to do something to people. There was wonderment, obviously, at a dog who had to bend down to pinch a steak off a kitchen counter, but there was also something so special about this amazing boy of ours. For want of a better word, we called it his 'aura'. It was, we decided, the same kind of special something that separated true movie stars from all the other actors.

And whatever it was, George enjoyed it. You could take him pretty much anywhere around people and he was happy. He might shower everyone around him in drool (as a consequence we never travelled anywhere these days without either one of our 'drool towels', or rolls of kitchen paper), but he was never once cranky or uptight, or skittish or bad-tempered — no wonder he was so much in demand.

During the holidays things had been pretty quiet — just as we'd planned — but after the break things really started to pick up. We got a call from the drug company Pfizer's Animal Health Division. Their annual convention was right here in Tucson and they wanted to know if George could come over to the hotel to do photos with the attending veterinarians.

The organisers were very professional right off, and set it up so that George would pose with small groups of doctors at a time. We did this a few times to accommodate all the attending doctors, and George didn't seem to mind in the least. Far from it — he seemed to have this sixth sense about when the 'say cheese!' moment happened. He'd always pose with such grace and stand perfectly still.

Back online, we knew things were still growing exponentially: for the month of January our website had over 30,000 visitors — an absolutely incredible number. And if we'd been thrilled to reach the magic number of one thousand fans on Facebook, we had even more excitement in store. By the end of the second week in January, we hadn't just doubled that figure — we were getting close on reaching *five* thousand.

Yes, we were responsible grown-ups with

day jobs, but we were all like a bunch of overexcited kids. Dana would go peek at Facebook when she should have been working, and fire off an email to Paul and me: '4,974!'. She didn't need to put anything else in the email — we knew what the numbers referred to.

And then that evening, she checked again, grabbed her cell and called Paul. 'Are you watching?' she wanted to know, before Paul could even say hello.

'Of course I'm watching!' he answered. '4,997!'

'You know what?' said Dana. 'If anyone could see us, up at 11 at night, hunched over our computers, doing what we're doing, they'd think we were mad!'

'Yeah, but isn't it fun?' Paul started to reply. 'Yey! Five thousand! We got it! We're rocking!'

And it didn't stop there. By the last day of January, George had a staggering 10,000 Facebook fans. And it wasn't just the number of people that amazed me; it was their enthusiasm, their interest, their real passion.

But if George's fans were on board, it seemed the Guinness organisation was not. We got a call from them, right at the beginning of February. 'I'm sorry,' the man said, 'but there's a problem.'

18

Every Dog Has His Day

I took the call and it really knocked me for six. The man was British — you could tell right away from his accent — and he explained that he was calling from London, from the Guinness World Records headquarters, in fact.

'A problem?' I asked him, once he'd explained who he was. 'I don't understand. What sort of problem?'

'I'm sure it's nothing to worry about,' he quickly reassured me. 'It's just that we've had someone get in touch by letter, and it seems there's some controversy about George's recorded height.'

I was stunned, but at the same time alarm bells began ringing. Would someone really go to such lengths to deny George the title? Was this the same person who'd made all those comments? It was incredible. Yet it seemed to be happening, even so. 'What sort of controversy?' I asked him. 'We followed all your protocols to the letter.'

'I'm sure you did,' he said soothingly. 'It's

just that someone has challenged the data you sent in and — '

'Challenged?' I asked him, my mind whirling now. How could someone be so fixated on this that they'd make so much effort to dispute the results? What had we ever done to them? 'Who has challenged it?' I wanted to know. 'How? On what grounds?'

The man seemed anxious to reassure me I mustn't worry, but at the same time he wasn't about to tell me. 'I'm sure you'll understand,' he said, 'and I'm really very sorry, but it's important that we are seen always to follow up this sort of thing. All we need is — '

I interrupted because I knew what was coming. 'For George to get measured again, right?'

'Exactly,' he confirmed. 'We're going to need a second measurement from a different veterinarian, just so we can corroborate your figures. Can you arrange that, do you think? And for the measurement we'll send one of our own adjudicators to verify the measurement and act as a witness. Is that okay?'

I said yes because really what choice did we have? We knew we'd done everything completely to the letter, but if they needed for us to do it all again, then so be it. It really didn't matter *who* was so intent on causing trouble. We certainly were living and learning!

We arranged that we'd sort something out for 10 February, when their adjudicator, Jamie Panas — who'd be flying all the way to Tucson from New York — could come down and confirm that we had measured George correctly.

'Unbelievable' was Christie's opinion, when I called and told her. 'And kind of sad, too, don't you think?'

'Sad?' I answered.

'Yes,' she said. 'I think it *is* sad. I mean, sad that this bitter person is so completely stuck on all this that they'd go to such lengths to cause trouble for us. He's just a pet. They all are. Like it really matters so much to them that they even write to Guinness? Like they really have so little else in their lives? It's incredible, that's what it is.'

★ ★ ★

But, incredible as it was, there was more incredulity to come.

''That's Incredible!''

I'd listened hard, but wasn't sure I heard that I'd heard right. 'I beg your pardon?'

''That's Incredible!' the woman who'd called my cell said again. 'You remember we spoke on the phone a couple months back? About George guesting on one of our 'That's

237

Incredible!' shows?'

I laid down my drill and carefully climbed down my ladder. It was 11 February and I was doing some work on a house that I was selling, a few miles from where we lived, close to downtown. I had a guy working with me on some wiring that needed doing, and what with the noise he was making across the room from me too, I'd missed the first couple of things the woman had said. But now I *could* hear and realisation kicked in. It was Shantel, the producer I'd talked to before, from *The Oprah Winfrey Show*.

'We're busy preparing the next one,' she explained again. 'And we wondered how you felt about bringing George along to guest on the show.'

George himself ambled up now and snorted at my cell. Was he really so clever that he could sniff the smell of celebrity? The whiff of fame? The heady scent of success? I smoothed a hand over his velvety head. The whole idea of George 'guesting' on a TV show seemed so funny. 'That sounds great in theory,' I said. 'Except you know what's been happening with all that, right?'

I didn't actually know she knew about it — I just assumed that she must know something. Why else would she be calling today? I explained about the challenge to our data that had come in, and the fact that Guinness needed us to measure George again.

'Which was supposed to happen yesterday, but didn't,' I added. 'The adjudicator's flight here got cancelled, because of all the snow in New York. So we had to rearrange the date. It's now scheduled to take place next Monday, the 15th.'

But I'd obviously been wrong about what the woman did and didn't know. It seemed she knew nothing of the whole re-measuring fiasco; they just wanted George on because they wanted George on. But now she *did* know, she was really excited about it. In fact, she was on a new mission.

'That's just *brilliant*,' she told me, and I could hear her shuffling papers. 'So, yes, let me see now. We need to be there too.'

'You do? At the measuring?'

'Yes, we do. Absolutely. So we can film it for the show. Just perfect. 15 February, you say? Next Monday?'

'Yup. Monday the 15th.'

'Okay. That's great. Now leave everything with me, Dave. I'll make a start on getting things organised right away. Oh, and, one thing: are you able to promise me something?'

'What?'

239

'That you won't appear on — or talk to — any other shows in the meantime? That's pretty important, as you can imagine, because this is potentially big news, and we want to be the ones to break it. Okay?'

'Of course. That's fine,' I said. 'No problems. But — '

'Because, obviously, if it's ratified and George *does* get the title, then we'll need to get him on up here to Chicago right away.'

'Yes, that's fine, as I say, but — '

'And we'd need him on his way to us within the next twenty-four hours after the measuring, ideally. Strike while the iron's hot!'

'Yes, of course, but — '

'I'm sorry?'

'But how are we going to *do* that?' I finally managed to cut in. 'I mean it's great and all, and I'm sure George would absolutely love all the attention, but how's he going to get from Tucson to Chicago? Because there's no way we're sticking him in a crate on a plane or driving him all the way across country.'

There wasn't even so much of a micro-second of silence. 'Oh,' she said breezily. 'No need for you to worry about that. We'll fly you all here first class, of course!'

★   ★   ★

Jamie, the Guinness official adjudicator, flew in from New York on Sunday, 14 February, at around 2 p.m. It was raining a little when Paul and I drove out to Tucson airport to collect her. Was that going to be some sort of omen?

We were both a bit nervous about meeting her, because we didn't know what to expect. New York. It had plenty of connotations, for sure. New Yorkers were a breed apart, weren't they? Paul had been there. I hadn't. But it made no real difference. New Yorkers were all hard-driven, in-your-face people, weren't they? Would *she* be like that? All high heels and sharp edges? Or would she be softer round the edges — a fun, fashionable New Yorker, like you saw in all the cable shows? Would she be an older woman — hell, she was a Guinness adjudicator, wasn't she? — who hated dogs and had no sense of humour? If so, then we might have trouble relating to her.

Tucson airport's not too big, and it's not too busy either, but even so, to show willing, we made a sign with her name on it, and stood in arrivals like a pair of nervous school kids waiting for someone they expected to be a bit scary. Ridiculous, but that's what it felt like that day — like she was some prim school principal who held our fate in her hands.

So it wasn't surprising that we almost missed her. As this glamorous blonde sashayed, smiling, towards us, we both, for a moment, did a double-take. This couldn't be her, could it? This good-looking, sophisticated young woman, with hair right off *America's Next Top Model*?

But it seemed it was, so I opened my arms to give her a welcome hug, as did Paul. We exchanged a glance. Yup. We both liked her.

'Nice and hot, at least,' she observed chattily, as we left the airport and made our way back out to the parking lot. She'd been flying for about six hours but looked like she meant business; she was fresh and friendly but also very professional, which was important.

We now had a whole lot riding on this trip. I'd lost count of the number of hours we'd put into the application; to have it fail at the last hurdle would be pretty disappointing for us all. We knew it made no great difference to our lives but ever since the allegation of foul play regarding our original figures, I was angry. If nothing else, I was determined to set things straight about that.

And though Jamie was real friendly, and we exchanged a bunch of pleasantries, whenever talk turned to our actual application, she was consistent in using one phrase in particular: it was always a case of '*if* George is tall enough . . . '

Paul and I exchanged looks through the rear-view mirror of my car. 'Yikes,' we said through eye contact. 'This is pretty serious.' I prayed that George would perform.

★   ★   ★

'So, this is it, then,' said Paul, after we'd dropped Jamie at her hotel. She'd opted for the Marriott, close to my house, and told us she didn't need to meet with us again until the morning. We had offered to take her out for a drink, or for some dinner — we thought she might like to meet the family, or meet George. But she'd been adamant. She had paperwork to catch up on, and she wanted to get some sleep before tomorrow's big event.

'Sure is,' I agreed, as we sat in the stationary car, in the hotel parking lot. I was a bit worried that her declining to meet George beforehand was because she didn't want to get *too* friendly, in case she had to dash our hopes. 'Funny,' I added, 'how much all this suddenly seems to matter, you know?'

'Sure do,' Paul agreed. 'Because it *does* matter. You know, Dave, I know this is going to sound a bit dramatic, but this whole thing has become a *really* big deal to me. To Dana, too. To all of us. Yeah, I know that it all started as just a bit of fun, something a bit different, but now . . . ' He shrugged. 'Now it's become such a lot more than that, hasn't it? It's been really . . . I don't know . . . invigorating? You know, creating the website, doing all the media stuff, exploring all the possibilities, dealing with the press. I mean I know it's not like a business or anything, and it's not about money, but on the other hand it *is*. It's been great doing something with so much potential. The kids are loving it, *we're* loving it — it's just so right up our alley. I haven't felt so energised by anything in years.'

'And you and Dana have done such a great job,' I pointed out. 'But can you imagine how big all this'll get if he gets it?'

'Big,' Paul said, nodding. 'Potentially, *so* big.'

We both sat in silence then, contemplating the concept of 'bigness', both of us still unsure, I think, what that might mean. Might George become a brand? Some sort of global ambassador? We'd already seen what a big draw he was for children around the world. I nodded. As projects went — and the whole Guinness thing *had* become a project — it had the potential for taking over whole chunks of our lives.

244

This made me think of Christie, and Annabel, and the time, and priorities. I started the engine. 'I'd better get on home, I guess.'

'Me too,' Paul said as we both exhaled at exactly the same time — like a couple of gladiators, psyching up before battle.

'So,' Paul said again. 'This is it, then.'

★　★　★

The night of the 14th was calm and uneventful. Christie and I had an early take-out from our favourite restaurant, and then I read *Goodnight Moon* to Annabel before she went to sleep, with George, now her big best friend, close by, heavy-eyed, on his mattress. It sometimes felt — and Christie had exactly the same feeling — that we were reading bedtime stories to them both.

I was as excited and as nervous as I'd been about anything in a long while, but I was also sensible enough not to drone on and on to Christie about Guinness. Despite her commitment to the cause — to getting George his rightful title — I wasn't so silly as to think my long-suffering and patient wife didn't have better things to talk about than my ever-expanding Guinness-related plans. These I saved for when I took George out for a quick stroll before bedtime, trying to imagine what a dog had to do once he was crowned — *if* he was crowned — Tallest Dog in the World.

'Maybe it'll be a bit like being crowned Miss Universe,' I told him as we sauntered along our usual route, past the usual crop of neighbours' houses, watching them doing all the stuff people did at that time of day. 'Opening galas,' I went on, 'making personal appearances, doing good works for charity. You'd enjoy that. And you're a natural in front of cameras,' I added. 'Though you obviously mustn't let it go to your head.'

George, who was making detours, grabbing the chance to get his paws among the grass and flowers, now pulled away to investigate a late-roving gecko he'd spotted, as if to remind me just how unlikely a scenario that would be. He was a dog with his paws planted very firmly on the ground. Just as well — if he accidentally trod on your foot these days, boy, did your foot know about it.

I stood and waited, musing beneath the star-strewn desert sky. The potential in all this, I knew, *was* incredible. Paul had it right: I felt energised too, excited. Fancy fate throwing something so unexpected into our lives? And whatever we did — however we chose to play it — *if* George got it, it was something we must deal with wisely.

246

★ ★ ★

We'd arranged for the second height verification to take place the following morning at the offices of another Tucson veterinarian, Dr James Boulay. He ran one of the largest and most well-respected vet clinics in the entire Southwest Arizona region, so, like our own guy, Doc Wallace, he was pretty busy. We were really grateful that he managed to find the time to fit us in, especially since we'd had to reschedule.

The plan was for Paul to pick Jamie up from her hotel first thing. He'd then take her straight on to the vet's office, while I'd bring George from home and meet them there. The drive from the hotel to Dr Boulay's was around twenty minutes, and, as Paul told me later, it was a pretty tense time. Jamie spent much of it on the phone to her headquarters, and the words '*if* George is tall enough' kept cropping up again. Paul began to fret for a second time. Was there something they weren't telling us? Was another dog now in the running? Did they not trust our figures? Would all my training pay off or had all that hard work been for nothing? Or — and this was beginning to feel increasingly like a possibility — could anything, even this late in the process, still go wrong? What about the

247

drizzle (it was raining *again* — completely out of character for Tucson)? Would it affect George? And would Dr Boulay, whom George had never met, scare him?

Happily, despite his worries, Paul used the time well. Jamie, as she'd explained to him, had yet to meet a Great Dane, let alone one as enormous as George. And, since she seemed nervous, Paul reassured her that George really was a gentle giant, and that she didn't need to worry in the least. As Jamie chatted on her cell, he also noticed something else — he could partially see into her open briefcase. Inside was a large custom-framed Guinness certificate, which naturally cheered him up no end. The only annoying thing was that he couldn't see the writing.

They arrived at the clinic around fifteen minutes before George and I did to help get the recently arrived *Oprah* camera crew ready, and to put Dr Boulay on standby. Jamie was still on her cell as she climbed out of Paul's car and, with her hands full — she was going through a bunch of official papers — she asked Paul to take her briefcase and 'don't lose it!'

Paul being Paul, and not one to miss an opportunity, took this one to have another quick peek at that frame. Happily, he saw what he'd hoped he would see: the words

'Tallest Dog' and 'Giant George' leapt right out. Clearly, the folk at Guinness — in the certificate department at least — were feeling more than cautiously optimistic.

But if Paul was feeling calmer, I wasn't. Though I was gratified to see Jamie grab his arm and squeak, 'Oh my God!' when she saw George, I was still privately worried about whether George would come up to the mark. As I set up the planks on my truck, I was all too aware that the activity around us — particularly the camera crew and their equipment — might prove a distraction. I was also aware, as Paul went into the clinic for Dr Boulay, that George was already getting real excited, seeing the planks piling on the tailgate, hopping from leg to leg, his mouth visibly watering; once he could sense chicken in the air you could really see it happening. But much as I wanted him to be prepped and ready, I didn't want him over-excited, as he had to stand still long enough to be measured.

I got everything in place behind the tailgate, George sniffing the air with increasing enthusiasm as the scent of the chicken finally hit his nostrils. Paul went in then, and came back moments later with Dr Boulay, who looked very official in his crisp white lab coat. We then needed to position George so that he was in the correct place for the ruler — a big measuring stick, around head height for George, with a crossbar that could be moved up and down. What was needed was for the doc and I to stand on either side of him and, as he went for the chicken, to move the crossbar into position so that it sat horizontally across his shoulders.

Jamie, who was watching, would then confirm the figure the doc called out, checking it herself to corroborate it.

It was fiddly, and it depended on George's complete cooperation. 'This had better not be the day he goes off chicken!' I thought, especially as there was so much other interesting stuff going on. But George didn't let me down — why'd I ever worry that he might? He *loved* chicken and he was going to stand up good and tall to get it; all the people around him didn't bother him one bit.

And so it was, moments later, that Jamie spoke the immortal words. Having confirmed the previous record as being forty-two and a quarter inches, she could confirm that, at forty-three inches, George was officially 'now the world's tallest dog'.

In true Georgie fashion, he wasn't the least bit interested. His only goal at this point was to make a quick beeline for the bit of meat he could see I had left in my little plastic box.

Jamie, at this point, had her back to George and me — she was having a quick chat with Dr Boulay, by the tailgate, while I took him round to help him back into the truck. The box was in my right hand and, such was his determination to get close to it, he pushed his way through the gap between Jamie and me.

'You see that?' hissed Paul, as we reached the driver's door.

'See what?' I asked, opening the box to persuade George to climb in.

'Jamie's *coat!*' he whispered. 'Look at the back of it!'

I looked. She was wearing a smart black tailored jacket — very classy, and now accessorised by a six-inch-long line of glistening drool.

And if there was a surprise for Jamie (though nothing the ubiquitous roll of kitchen paper couldn't rectify), there was another surprise in store for us too. Though it had never crossed our minds that there was another record up for grabs, Jamie told us that George was not only the World's Tallest Living Dog, but also the World's Tallest Dog *Ever*. Not that George cared how many records he had; he was just happy about the chicken.

For the rest of us, though, it was one great big relief, and incredibly exciting. Paul immediately called Dana — who'd been unable to get the time off work — while I got straight on my cell to tell Christie and, of course, Shantel from *The Oprah Winfrey Show*.

But that had to be the end of us talking about it, because we were officially embargoed by *Oprah*. That was the deal — we had promised to talk to no one. So we couldn't do anything to celebrate. We couldn't update the website, couldn't tweet on Twitter, couldn't update our Facebook status — couldn't do anything. We had to keep mum about everything because that's what we'd promised. It was Oprah who would have the job of telling America that George was officially the 'Tallest Dog in the World Ever', not to mention being the 'Tallest Living Dog'.

It made the whole thing feel a bit of an anticlimax, but not for long. Now we had to get busy — and how. We had a trip to Chicago to prepare for . . .

19

Love Me, Love My Dog

'First class?' Christie spluttered. 'But I thought you were joking when you said that! They're really going to fly us all to Chicago first class?'

I nodded. 'Honey, I am absolutely not kidding you.' I gestured to my cell and the call I'd just disconnected. 'Honestly, that's what she just said.'

'All of us? Really?'

I nodded again. '*All* of us. One seat for you, one for me, two for Georgie — '

'Two for *Georgie*?'

I grinned. 'Yup, they think George will need two seats, apparently.'

She glanced at him now, and he cocked his head sideways, as if to say, 'You got a problem with that, Mom?'

'Well,' she said, finally. 'I am pretty impressed. I was thinking they'd expect him to sit on the floor. Wow. Who'd have imagined this?' She shook her head. 'First class to Chicago. Wow. In fact, first class to anywhere! How exciting is that, Dave? I mean, wow!'

★   ★   ★

It had been a case of 'wow' pretty much since we'd said goodbye to Jamie that morning, and George and I had headed home from Dr Boulay's office followed by the whole *Oprah* film crew.

It wasn't simply a question of us appearing on the show, apparently; they also had to film some additional footage, called a b-roll, which would introduce us — and show George in his normal home environment — as the forerunner to our segment on the show.

As afternoons went, ours was fast becoming surreal. Sure, we'd done filming before — the stuff we'd put on YouTube, and the original measuring — but this was serious; these were professionals at work, and they took their job very, very seriously.

Luckily, I was never a shy kind of guy, but even I was a little fazed at being professionally 'directed', as they had me and George open our front door, had me inviting the viewers in, had us parading around the house, showing off his food bowls and his bed. But if I was a little self-conscious about it, George himself was entirely unfazed. Hell, he was the tallest dog in the world now, *officially*. Because this was to be shown before we went on camera in Oprah's studio to have the

254

official Guinness announcement made, I had to make a small adjustment to the script, and just say that I *thought* he was.

That done, while Christie got on the phone to her boss to arrange a couple of days' leave, we all headed down to the dog park. They wanted to film George running about with his friends, and also thought it would be cool if I could bring down my enormous, home-improvised pooper-scooper. 'You need big tools for big jobs!' I quipped to camera.

It was now around 4.00 in the afternoon — several hours since either Christie or I had had a chance to grab ourselves a meal but, at the same time, less than six since the measuring had taken place — and already the colossal *Oprah Winfrey Show* machine was in full flow. It was like we'd been swept up by some huge TV juggernaut — all-powerful, and completely unstoppable.

But I wasn't worried. Right off, it felt that every single thing would be taken care of, right down to the *Oprah* show detailing by an amazing lady, Shantel, who'd already put all sorts of things in motion. She'd even organised an appointment for George to see Doc Wallace, so he could get a certificate to confirm he was fit to fly. I'd headed off to the vet with him right after the crew left.

And her next mission — the reason she had

called me now — was to get George and us from Tucson to Chicago by airplane, preferably tomorrow.

It didn't seem to matter to the Oprah team just how hard that might be to achieve in practice, and, as she'd explained to me on the phone, it had been proving pretty hard. Since we'd last spoken about it — right after the measuring took place — there'd been quite some job on back in Chicago, apparently, to solve the problem of how best they could get George to the show.

They'd first suggested transporting him via a pet charter. A pet charter is a flight that takes animals only, in crates, and has no seats on board for any passengers. This was complex and far from ideal. First, because we'd have to dovetail it with another flight for me and Christie, and second, because we weren't so sure George would enjoy being crated up and separated from us for that length of time. As it turned out, a pet charter wouldn't work anyway. It was only good for pets up to a hundred and fifty pounds — a whole ninety-five pounds less than George was.

Next up, then, was the plan to hire a private jet for him. But costing close to a staggering $30,000, this was dismissed as being a little *too* much, even for *The Oprah Winfrey Show* to fork out. Since then they'd contacted several of the big airlines, without success. This latest call from Shantel had brought good news, however. Apparently, American Airlines were up for trying to do it — and first class — but only if a long list of boxes were ticked, including George wearing a muzzle so he wouldn't scare the other passengers. They were also worried about how flying might affect him. Would he vomit? Would his ears hurt? Would he be scared and get aggressive? Would he lose control and go to the bathroom on the plane?

These were all real concerns, and they had every right to voice them. It was a big deal taking *any* animal into the air in a plane, let alone when that animal's the size of a large lion, and in the cabin with the passengers. I told Shantel to reassure them that he really was a gentle giant, that he had a bladder capacity that could probably bust a few world records of its own, and that I didn't doubt for a second that he'd deal with air travel the same way he dealt with everything else — without the least bit of fuss.

She called the airline back, but they weren't satisfied. They weren't happy about doing it unless they felt reassured, and they felt they would be only if they could meet George beforehand, which was why Shantel had just called me back. Could I maybe get myself and George down to Tucson airport to meet with someone from AA? Give the thing a bit of a try out — like, now?

'So George and I have to head down to the airport,' I told Christie, 'to give Project Oprah a dry run.'

'What, *now*?' she said, glancing at the kitchen clock in shock.

'Yup,' I confirmed. 'Like, *now*.'

★   ★   ★

As George and I headed off in my truck to the airport, I took some time to take it all in. We were now the owners of the tallest dog in the world, ever. The tallest dog in the *whole world*. It was mind blowing. It was incredible to think that all the hard work had paid off, that our pet was now famous — potentially *world* famous.

'Hey, Georgie,' I said. 'How does it feel, now it's official? Do you feel different? Do you feel special? Do you feel ready for your fifteen minutes of fame?'

I shook my head. Fame. What a strange concept for a dog, and one that obviously, bar a whole load of petting and attention, meant nothing to George whatsoever. And he was going to be a 'celebrity passenger', courtesy of Oprah Winfrey and American Airlines

— well, more correctly, a celebrity passenger if it all worked out okay. Would he really be as cool as I'd reassured everybody he would be? Would he do okay at 39,000 feet? Would he be okay as a guest on a TV show?

I glanced across at him as we drove, and he glanced right on back. Yup, he seemed to say, he'd be just *fine*.

Shantel had arranged for us to meet a guy at the airport — he was the local head manager for American Airlines, based in Tucson, and it was he who had to decide whether everything was going to work. It took around thirty minutes for us to get there, and by the time we arrived it was dark. The drizzly clouds of earlier had disappeared, too, and the sky was, as ever, full of stars.

I love airports at night, the light and the sprawl of them, the fact that everyone's heading somewhere, that feeling of expectation and excitement they always seem to have. And this was something different in itself. As it was the airline manager's day off, he'd come from home specially to do this. He'd brought his wife along, too, as she was so keen to meet George, so, once we'd found them, we spent some time out on the forecourt taking pictures.

We left her then, and went into the bowels of the airport, which gave me a real feeling of déjà vu. We were heading to a different area in a different airport, but it felt just like when we'd come to pick up George as a puppy all that time ago at the airport in Phoenix, as we went through a whole bunch of corridors and elevators that you'd never know existed, and then suddenly — *voilà!* — we were out on the back side, and there was this great big AA airplane just sitting there.

'So, how is he with travelling generally?' the guy, who was called Pete, asked me, as we crossed the tarmac towards it.

'Oh, just fine,' I answered. 'Provided he has room. I mean, he hasn't flown anywhere since he was a puppy, of course — '

He nodded. 'Shantel mentioned. And I'm with you, there. It'd be one hell of a thing for him to travel in the hold. Is there even a crate anywhere that would hold him?' He laughed then, and shook his head. 'Stupid question. I'm guessing that's a 'no'!'

I nodded. 'But on road trips, he's always been great. He's real placid, as you can see, and he's a great sleeper. Plus he has this truly amazing bladder. It's incredible, really. He can go all day and night if he needs to.'

'All day *and* night? That's incredible. So no worries on a four-hour flight, then.'

'None at all.'

But he didn't look as though he was convinced.

* * *

It was really weird, getting on a big empty plane, just Pete, me and George — not that George was bothered. As perhaps befitted a dog whose diet included several pounds of Paul Newman's finest dog food every week, he trotted right on up the steps, every inch the matinee idol, and even turned left, towards the first-class area, when he got to the top. It was as though he *knew* which part of the cabin was the part he should be in.

'Okay,' said Pete, as I followed him down the fuselage, taking in the space, and the feeling of opulence. There were two seats on each side of the central aisle, with loads of leg space between them. And they were big seats too — way bigger than the ones we were used to in coach, with large armrests and headrests, all made of fine leather.

'So,' he said. 'Here's the first-class cabin. We were thinking that if we sat George in here . . . ' he gestured. 'You and your wife can sit across the aisle from him.' He pointed out a row. 'You want to try him in here?'

'Sure,' I said. I tried every which way I could think of to fit him in. I tried him rear first, backing him into the row of seats, and then I tried him forwards so his head faced the window. I tried him on the seats (Pete

261

didn't seem to mind this at all), then I tried him in front of the seats, sitting on the floor. But there was simply no way we could do it. However George settled himself — and he seemed to be loving this new game of ours — there just wasn't room for him to fit. He was too big. The set-up at the front simply wasn't wide enough for him. If he lay down — which is what he'd be doing, pretty much — his head not only stuck out into the aisle, it stuck out so far that his paws were touching the seat across the aisle. And they couldn't have that for safety reasons, of course, not to mention it would impede the trolley that brought all the goodies.

'Okay,' Pete said finally, having watched all these attempts with a wry expression on his face. 'I don't think this is going to work, is it?' he shook his head. 'You're not going to want to hear it, I know, but I think it might have to be economy after all.'

So we filed back to economy, and it seemed to me he was right. There was plenty more width to play with here. What George probably needed was the row at the bulkhead — the row immediately behind the partition and galley, where there was plenty of floor space in front of the seats too. Here he could stretch out properly. Back here it was also set up with three seats on one side and two on the other, and, as we'd thought, the three side was perfect for him. Christie and I could have the bank of two opposite. We had George try it out, and, hey presto, it worked fine.

Or at least, I thought it did. I could see that Pete wasn't so sure. It was a feeling I'd had pretty much since we'd started this whole process. Though he was pleasant and friendly, the whole tone of this operation had felt serious from the start. Much as I was doing my best to reassure him, I knew that if he didn't feel it would work to take George on this aircraft, then there was no way he was going to okay it.

'I don't know,' he said, shaking his head. 'This all still seems a bit tight to me. I'm not sure they're going to go for this.'

The 'they' in this case were the higher powers at AA, who were in charge of safety, and Pete explained that he'd need to talk to them before they could give things the all clear. I got the impression that there was quite a lot riding on this, that this decision was quite a big responsibility for him. He'd already taken a couple of photos of George in first class, and now he took a couple more of him sitting in the bulkhead. 'You know,' I said, as he did so, wanting to reassure him some more, 'you can trust me on this. George really is *the* most chilled dog on the planet.

And he's trained, so he's highly obedient, too.

'I don't doubt that,' he told me, as we went back down the steps. 'And I will do my best on this, I promise. But I really don't know. I can't get you an answer right now. We'll be back to you — well, Shantel will, I guess — just as soon as we can.'

We made uncomfortable small talk as he escorted us out, my mind mainly elsewhere as it was beginning to sink in that the chances were high this wouldn't happen. We finally reached the public area of the airport again. There was nothing I could do now except keep my fingers crossed, and with the flight time tomorrow morning now less than twelve hours away, I just had to hope for the best. I thanked Pete, and made one last stab at reassuring him, then George and I headed back towards town.

As I drove, the whole exercise was beginning to feel crazy, and I wondered if the chances of the trip happening were disappearing fast. Here George and I were running around town late on a Monday evening, and the whole thing could be for nothing. But we had to keep positive that it would happen; fingers crossed, Pete would come through for us with the airline. While he did what he had to do, we had a job of our own. We had to get to a pet store and buy a muzzle for

George before the stores closed for the night. I hadn't realised how late it was, so we had only a few minutes to get to the nearest pet store, but we had to make it, because no muzzle meant *definitely* no flight.

Happily, we made good time through the evening traffic, and arrived at PetCo, a five-minute drive from home, just before it closed. George and I jumped out of the truck and pretty much dived through the entrance. Having cruised down several aisles as they were turning out all the lights, we eventually found and grabbed the biggest muzzle we could find. It still didn't look big enough, I thought anxiously, as I paid for it, but it was all the store had, so it would have to do.

'It's definitely not big enough,' Christie said when we got home and I showed it to her. 'We're going to have to work out a way to make it bigger.'

'How can we?' I asked her. I was really beginning to stress now.

'Give it to me,' she said, reaching in the kitchen drawer for some scissors. 'I'm sure I can work out a way to do it if I think long enough. Why don't you head off and get your things packed?'

★   ★   ★

As every new parent will probably tell you, once you have your first baby almost everything you do suddenly feels like a major military operation. One minute you can come and go as you please, the next every single trip — even if it's to the store for a carton of milk — feels like it has to be organised to a huge degree. In the early days with Annabel, on occasions when I had her on my own, it sometimes felt like I'd rather go without pretty much anything I needed than have to do everything I had to do to get myself and my tiny baby organised to go out — get her diapered, dressed, into the car, out of the car, into her buggy, into a store, out of the store, back into the car, home, out of the car and back to wherever we'd started. And we lived in Arizona — how did people manage (and I clearly remember thinking this) who lived in cold places like Alaska?

And if those sorts of trips had seemed like military operations, what we had to do now felt ten times more complicated. If we were going to make that flight in the morning, we had a lot to do in a short space of time. As well as packing for ourselves, we had to get everything sorted for George, of course — a whole bunch of his favourite food, portioned out, meal by meal, in zip-lock bags, as well as a few doggie treats, his drool towels (we

266

packed several, in case the colour of them mattered for the cameras), his leash, his food and water bowls, and a bunch of big — and I mean BIG — bags for his giant poops. Then we had to get everything packed for Annabel too, because Christie had arranged that we'd drop her around to my parents, who'd look after her for the two days we'd be away. It would be longer, in fact, because we'd planned to drop her that night — it made so much more sense to do that than to get her up so early and have to take her there on our way to the airport in the morning, even though — and I knew Christie was stressing about this too — it would be the first night she'd ever spent away from us.

I went into the bedroom to see much of the job all but done, though; while George and I had been at the airport, Christie had been busy too. She'd got the half ton of stuff for Annabel pretty much sorted: the travel cot, the buggy, all the diapers and changing gear. It looked like she'd be staying with my mom and dad for a month. I got on and started grabbing my own things.

'Hey,' said Christie, following me in a few minutes later, with Annabel at her hip and George at her side. He was modelling the now butchered giant-sized muzzle and looking reassuringly cool about it all. 'I think this'll work, if we stitch it, don't you?' She'd cut the bottom seam through to make the whole thing much bigger, and from somewhere she'd managed to find some strips of Velcro, which she'd pinned into place to try out for size. 'I'm thinking that if we restitch it all with the strips underneath, it'll be big enough, but also stay closed. What d'you think?'

I shook my head, surveying both the time and my little family. It seemed crazy to be running around doing all this stuff when we still didn't know if it was going to happen. It was almost ten on a chilly Monday evening in February, and at least four out of the four of us should be in bed, not stitching muzzles and packing for a siege, much less depositing our daughter at my folks' at what might turn out to be midnight, then heading off at dawn to Chicago. If that, indeed, was what it would turn out we *were* doing.

'This thing is getting more surreal by the minute,' I said. 'But, yes. Great job. That'll do fine, hon.'

As if on cue, my cell barked only seconds later. It was Shantel. It seemed we were good to go.

20

It's a Small World After All

So much for keeping everything quiet.

When we arrived at Tucson airport at 5 a.m. on Tuesday, we got our first proper taste of what was to come. It seemed the whole world and his wife were there with us — well, not the whole world, obviously, but a huge crowd of people, around a hundred and fifty of them at least, all of them waiting to catch the same flight as us, and all of them understandably a bit confused by the presence of a very big dog in their midst. You don't often see pet dogs in airports. And to see a dog as big as George must have been some sight — there was none bigger than he was and that was official.

Naturally, he quickly became the centre of attention. What was he doing there? Where were we all going? And, while we were at it, did we have a saddle for that thing?

We tried our best to be vague, and must have sounded it too. We just kept saying that the three of us 'had business in Chicago', which must have raised a heap more questions than it answered. But, hey, this was celebrity life, wasn't it?

★　★　★

After dropping Annabel at my mom and dad's the previous night, the pair of us had hardly slept a wink. We were excited, for sure — this was going to be one great adventure — but mostly it was because so much had happened in such a short space of time, and we were having a job keeping up with it all.

Luckily, I was working on our own house at that time, so taking some time out didn't matter too much, but Christie couldn't be off for more than a couple of days, as she had meetings and deadlines and customers to see, and needed to keep in touch by cell, too.

Unlike the two of us, however, George had been as chilled as could be. Sure, he was having a pretty good time at the moment, with so much fuss being made of him, so many unexpected and unlikely excursions, but as life was pretty much one long party for him anyway, he'd chowed down his dinner, gone to the bathroom in the backyard, flopped down on his bed and gone right off to sleep.

So he was fresh when we hit the airport, and raring to go. Raring to meet anyone who wanted to stroke and pet him, and suddenly there was a whole bunch of people — complete strangers — who seemed to want to do just that. So he lapped it all up while we fielded the questions, and made slow progress along to security. It was lucky we were early, because by the time we got through, we'd been meeting and greeting for over half an hour. But when we finally reached the security area, it soon became clear that our trip — now confirmed and about to happen — might be in jeopardy after all.

Once at the security gate, we were introduced to a number of people who'd been assigned the task of showing us through. The only thing was that there seemed to be a problem with the paperwork, as the TSA (Transportation Safety Administration, I think that stands for) required that there was an ID for every single seat booked. And since there was only one George but George had three seats, they were two out of three IDs short. There was a huddled conversation between the various officials, then the duty manager who'd escorted us told us to wait at security while he went back to his office to try and sort things out.

So we waited, and we waited, and we waited a little more. The other passengers continued to pet George as they passed us, and Christie and I made small talk with the security guys, while privately wondering if we'd spent half the day and night packing for nothing. Eventually, though, we spotted the manager in the distance, and after another round of conversation and much checking of bits of paper, George and Christie and I were allowed through.

But it seemed our pre-flight problems weren't quite over. We'd been asked to hang back till everyone else had boarded, so that we could make life easier for all by being the last on the plane. I also knew it was time to put on the muzzle — the muzzle that George had been fine with only a few hours ago, but which now it seemed he'd taken a violent dislike to. As soon as he saw it, and I tried to put it on him, he made his dislike of it plain. He started swinging his head from side to side to try and avoid it, tossing it this way and that, clearly annoyed with us.

We were both a bit dumbstruck. How could this have happened?

'But he was fine with it!' I hissed to Christie, hoping no one was seeing this. 'He didn't do this when we put it on him last night!'

'Yes, but perhaps he's doing this *because* we put it on him last night,' she hissed back. 'And he's remembering he didn't like it a whole lot!'

But the gods were being kind, because after making his point it seemed Georgie decided he'd roll with it anyway. Perhaps he could smell some chicken cooking in the galley — who knows? All we knew was that we were pretty relieved to have him finally muzzled up and good to board. We hurried down the jetway to the plane.

When you get on a plane, I guess the last thing you expect to see is an animal, and perhaps the *very* last thing would be an animal the size of George. So it was no surprise the first-class passengers, most of whom hadn't seen him yet, were stunned when he walked down the aisle. Some looked so in shock to see George saunter past to take his 'seat' that it was like we'd strolled on board with a tiger.

It was interesting just looking at their faces. Some looked on in amazement, obviously thinking this was pretty cool, but others looked scared. You could almost see their minds working, and imagine them thinking, 'Jeez, we're going to be on board with this animal for *four hours*?' Some looked so unsettled that I began to feel bad — flying was stressful enough for some people; how much more stress were they feeling right now?

But once we got settled and organised

ourselves, I realised I didn't need to worry. I could see a guy with a laptop, who was typing furiously, and then, suddenly, George's big beautiful face filled the screen. He then opened up his email, and I watched as he typed: *'That dog is on the plane with us right now!!!!'* We both felt much better after seeing that.

We took off on schedule, and I decided to take a chance on the muzzle. George was chilled as could be, so we removed it. We'd kind of figured things would be pretty quiet at this point, and that George would mostly nap his way through the flight. But what were we thinking? How naive were we!

Right away, there was an exodus to the front of economy, as everyone began making their way up the aisle, those who had met George to come see how he was getting on, and those who hadn't to come take a look for themselves at this huge dog they'd been told was on board. Once again, George lapped up all the attention. Why wouldn't he? He loved every minute. And though we'd been concerned about the three flight attendants, it seemed they loved him too, and were amazed at what a good boy he was.

'He's just incredible!' said one, which made Christie and me smile.

But as the flight got underway we started to

worry that George might be getting a little too much of a good thing. He'd lie down and get settled and then someone would come along, so he'd sit right back up again to soak up the attention. After a while, one of the flight attendants, seeing what was happening, asked us if we needed her to help calm things down.

We felt bad — we didn't want to offend anyone, much less stop anyone who still wanted to meet him — but she was right: it *was* too much. George needed to rest. So she went and put the 'fasten seatbelt' signs back on, so we could have a chance to relax. And we did: all three of us immediately dozed off.

★   ★   ★

But if we were shocked by the attention George was getting on the plane, it was nothing compared to what greeted us when we finally touched down in Chicago.

Despite all we'd been told about everyone keeping things secret, someone somewhere had obviously tipped someone else off because right away — almost as soon as we stepped off the airplane — there was another bunch of people, about a hundred this time, both employees of the airline and members of the public, and loads of cameras clicking.

But this time we experienced a new phenomenon: no one came up close to pet George; they all kept their distance and gawked from afar. It was like he was a movie star working a red carpet: he turned this way and that, head held high, really posing. And everyone stood and looked at him in awe.

'I don't know what it is,' I said to Christie, 'but that dog of ours has got it. Look at him! It's like he knows who he is! Like he's lapping up what he *knows* is his due.'

It was, too. There was this presence, this aura about him, a kind of vibe that seemed to bounce off him and was incredible to watch. I held the leash, sure, but it was George who was leading the action. Nothing could get in his way. It was a real esoteric thing, this star quality he exuded. You see it in certain movies stars — some have it in spades, some not so much. But it was what Christie and I were now seeing in our dog, and it was something else to witness.

★ ★ ★

But stars need their rest, especially before a big premiere, so we had to drag a reluctant George away from the circle of his clearly adoring fans. An AA manager greeted us and escorted us out of the airport, taking us and the driver, who'd come inside to meet us, straight to a limo — a limo! — that was waiting outside and would take the three of us straight to our hotel.

George loved that limo — and how. He was up and into it like it was exactly what he'd expected, hopping right up onto the long seat that ran the length of it, stretching out languidly and looking right at home. But however comfortable he looked, I was still a bit anxious, because despite all my confident talk about the size of his bladder, I was worried he might need the bathroom. He wasn't showing signs of any obvious distress, but, even so, when I asked the driver to stop and we got out, it was soon clear I'd been absolutely right. That done, we made the rest of the forty-minute journey, enjoying the sights of a city we'd both visited in summer, but which looked so gloriously different on this crisp winter's day.

They'd given us a room in the Omni Chicago Hotel, a really classy place right in the heart of downtown, where we could rest until we were due to be picked up early the next day. Till then, after the panics of the previous day and evening, all we wanted to do was veg out in front of the TV, order room service and sleep.

Once again, when we arrived outside the

hotel, we were given a great reception. We were escorted inside via a special back entrance, like they do with the President so there's not a huge fuss. And what a room it turned out we'd been given. We'd assumed it would be nice — it was a pretty nice hotel, after all. But when the guy opened the double doors and showed us inside, I think all our jaws dropped, including George's. It was huge. And so opulent, a real palace of a place and a million miles away from that Phoenix hotel where we'd been holed up with George when Christie had lost the baby. Here he was actually the guest of honour.

'It's the Governor's Suite, sir,' the guy explained proudly.

And it was certainly fit for a governor. It was fit for a king. It was massive, with a huge sitting room, a separate grand bedroom, an en suite you could hold a small party in, if you wanted to, a bar area, a dining area . . . it was amazing. But then we realised there was a fly in the ointment in all this high-living: there was no place in the suite for George to sleep.

'Tell you what,' said the desk clerk, when we called him with our problem, 'I'll have someone come right up with a roll-away bed for him.'

We thanked him and got on with the

all-important business of calling home to check on Annabel and working out what we wanted from room service. It was some menu, and the choosing would take time.

Minutes later, the roll-away was duly delivered, we tipped the bellboy and started to set it up.

'It's a bit small, isn't it?' was Christie's considered opinion, once we'd pulled off the sheets and pillows and blankets and coaxed George to climb up and give it a try. She grimaced as it seemed to quiver gently beneath him.

'And I'm not sure it's going to take his weight either.'

'We need to put the mattress on the floor,' I agreed. So we pulled the mattress off, rolled up the bed frame, cleared the blankets, and relocated the mattress to the floor.

We both looked and shook our heads once again.

'We need another roll-away, don't we?'

Christie got back on the phone, this time to order some supper and wine for us and another roll-away for Georgie. The guy who came up — the same one — looked at us like we were mad, but we didn't care. The star needed his sleep.

As did we. We gazed lovingly at the huge, fluffy king in the master bedroom. We would sleep well tonight.

We removed the bedding from the second roll-away and pulled off the second mattress, lining it up lengthways beside the first one.

'Hey, Georgie,' said Christie. 'Come try this out, will you? It's not perfect, I know, but it's oh so much better.' George tried it. He turned circles, turned some more, then flopped down.

'Sorted,' I said, as we heard a soft knocking at the door. 'Time for our dinner now, I think.'

I'd ordered steak and Christie had ordered salmon, accompanied by a bottle of Silver Oak Cabernet. It was a real treat, because the prices here were way higher than in Tucson, but as we'd been told that Oprah would foot the bill for us, it was fair to say we were very much looking forward to our meal — even more so once it was set up at the elegant table by the fire. We were ready to tuck in.

And we did, but we weren't long into our meals when Christie paused and nodded towards Georgie. 'He looks uncomfortable on that,' she said. 'Hon, do you think he looks uncomfortable?'

I looked across at him. And yes, he did look pretty uncomfortable. The two mattresses, being roll-away ones, were pretty thin, and even pushed together they weren't wide enough for him. Infuriatingly, they wouldn't stay together, either. He had his head on one mattress and his back end on the other, but his stomach was sagging onto the carpet.

'Yup,' I agreed, putting a forkful of steak into my mouth. 'You're right. That looks pretty uncomfortable.'

'Maybe, after we finish dinner,' Christie decided, 'we could move that chair over there — ' she raised a hand and pointed 'to stop the mattresses from sliding apart.'

'Good idea,' I said. 'And maybe we could shove those pillows against the head end. That'll at least give us a little bit more length to play with.'

'Good idea,' Christie agreed. 'That'll probably do it.'

Except it didn't, and right after we finished our dinner, we spent a frustrating half-hour, George looking on patiently, trying to manoeuvre things to make a bed for him that was both wide enough for his bulk and wouldn't move. The trouble was that every time he moved, the mattresses moved too. It was hopeless. Even bordered by the chair, it was hopeless. The mattresses were just so thin and bendy that they crumpled up under his weight.

I felt so sorry for him, I handed him a piece of my steak. 'You know what we *really* need to do?' I said in jest (I'd had that wine now, of course). 'We really need to give Georgie *our* bed to sleep on, and have the two roll-aways in this room ourselves.'

Christie looked at me, and I could see I'd made a fatal error. She didn't realise I was *joking* — not at all.

'You're absolutely right,' she said, hauling herself back up. 'D'oh! Why didn't we think of that in the first place?! Come on, let's get these beds sorted out.'

An hour later and the three of us were done for the night. We'd gathered up the mattresses, remade both of the roll-aways, put the stray bits of furniture back in the right positions, got undressed, cleaned our teeth and crawled into separate beds, where, from our pair of puny, thin roll-away mattresses, we stayed awake plenty long enough to see our boy go to sleep. He was lying sprawled, eyes rolled up in blissful doggie-dreaming, in the huge, fluffy king-size in the Governor's Suite of the terrifically swanky Omni Chicago Hotel.

'Well,' whispered Christie, as her roll-away creaked beneath her. 'It *is* George who is the star here, after all.'

21

Showtime

You know you've arrived when you get your own green room — not that we were sure what it was we'd arrived at, exactly. Playing a pair of chaperones to a superstar felt a pretty lofty place to be, though.

Neither Christie nor I had ever been near a TV studio before, so the whole experience blew us away. But the people at *Oprah* were lovely. They made everything so nice for us, right down to allocating the room for our personal use and making a huge comfy bed on the floor for George to rest on; and, in case we were hounded by over-enthusiastic fans, they'd even gone so far as to make a sign for the door. The sign said: 'Unless you are a member of Team Giant George, please don't ask to see him till taping is over.' And pretty much everyone ignored it.

Not that we minded, and George didn't either. They told us he was more popular with the staff at the studios than most of A-list Hollywood actors and actresses who passed through the show's hands.

As they would, I guess — everyone knew that an appearance on *The Oprah Winfrey Show* was just about the best publicity ticket ever, because the show, which has been going for around a quarter of a century, was simply the biggest, most famous talk show in the whole of America, not to mention the rest of the developed world. No wonder celebrities scrambled over one another to get a place on her sofa. So, when you thought about it, the people who worked on the show — and there were lots of them — must have been pretty used to having this movie star or that sports star show up with their entourage and their demands for this and that.

But here, in our Georgie, they'd found a real people's hero. And a perfect guest, too: one who hadn't arrived primed with a long list of riders; one who counted himself happy just to have his ears scratched. No wonder they loved him so much.

★　★　★

It had been another early start. We'd woken early — unsurprisingly, given our night on the roll-aways — and I'd taken George out for a walk, so he could go to the bathroom before we left. There was still plenty of snow around, but not so much that he got twitchy about where he was stepping; the sidewalks were mostly clear, and the bulk of the snow sat in big grubby piles at the road edge. That done, and after a quick room-service breakfast, the three of us were in reception at 7.30 sharp, waiting for the driver who'd take us to the studios. Another day, another limo. 'This is surreal,' Christie said. She was right. I had butterflies in my stomach — a first for maybe twenty plus years.

It *was* surreal, too. It was a world away from our lives in Arizona, both in terms of where we were and what we were doing. It seemed incredible to think that we were off to one of the most famous TV studios in the States.

Both the studio itself and the Oprah Winfrey production company are called Harpo — which is 'Oprah' spelt backwards, of course. It's the only studio complex in the world (I went online and found out this fact before we left home) that's owned by an African-American woman. Oprah Winfrey, in short, is a legend.

The studios were on Washington Boulevard, in Near West Side, about a twenty-minute drive from the Omni. Though I was feeling nervous, at least it wasn't going out live — the show would be taped today to be aired the following Monday, so I reassured myself that if George or I made any bloopers it maybe wouldn't be so bad. Even so, as I saw the big Harpo Studios sign in the distance, my nerves racked up a notch or four.

★   ★   ★

Shantel was there to greet us and welcome us to the studios, and she was as great in the flesh as she'd been on the phone. Right away you could see why she did what she did; she was in her thirties, I guess, and just oozed warmth and confidence. She hugged us both warmly and couldn't get over George; you could see right away she was a real dog lover.

Our green room was lovely, and very starry. The bed for George was a thoughtful touch, and there was a whole bunch of stuff — fruit, fresh coffee, dainty pastries and soft drinks, which we were encouraged to dive right into. Neither Christie nor I were hungry, but George eyed the pastries.

'Oh, no you don't, Georgie,' Christie warned him. His expression in response to this mild caution was wonderful to see. It said, 'Hell, Mom, I'm the star here, okay?'

'Right,' Shantel told us, 'this is what's going to happen. We're going to go down now and do a dry run in the studio — get George used to what's down there, all the people and cameras and stuff, okay? We find it helps to get everyone acclimatised to it. It can seem a little daunting if you've not been in a studio before.'

She was right, too. Leaving Christie in the green room, George and I went down some stairs and along a bunch of long corridors, and eventually found ourselves in this cavernous hangar, the middle bit of which I recognised from TV, except that it seemed to be made of chocolate!

'Oh, that's one of the segments,' Shantel explained, sounding like a TV set made of candy was nothing particularly out of the ordinary. 'The whole set behind us — ' she cast an arm around her 'is made out of Godiva chocolate. 70% cocoa solids, of course,' she added, grinning while I looked at it in amazement.

But even taking all that in, the place was amazing. It was such a massive operation. Behind the scenes — or more correctly, behind the chocolate scenery — was this whole mishmash of cameras, enormous great cameras, set on trollies that moved like the Daleks from the *Doctor Who* show in the UK, as well as bright lights and cables, like a writhing mass of serpents, and people wearing walkie-talkies and oversized headphones, pointing, hugging clipboards and running everywhere.

There was no audience at this stage. They'd be coming along later. But with what looked to be around fifty or so staff in the studio, it felt pretty packed as it was. And hot. How on earth would all that chocolate hold up? Once again, though, I was amazed by how relaxed Georgie was; he just strode around with me, sat as directed and stood up again, without it ever feeling in the least like he was antsy about anything. He was one amazingly cool dude.

The dry run done, we headed back to the green room so we could relax until it was time to tape the show itself.

'Will we meet Oprah beforehand?' I asked Shantel, as we departed.

She shook her head. 'No. Oprah doesn't like to meet her guests — whoever they are — until the minute they join her on the sofa. We like to do it that way so that her first interaction really *is* her first interaction. It keeps it fresher and more real that way.'

But if we didn't meet Oprah before we went into the studio, we met just about everyone else there. Despite the sign, there was a steady stream of staff coming to say hi to us, from the lowliest juniors to the Harpo bigwigs — everyone wanted to have their photo and their cuddle, seemingly oblivious to the fact that they'd all been told they weren't supposed to — but it was absolutely fine by us.

The last thing I had to do before the taping was to go to make-up — something more suited to Christie, to my mind, but as it had been me who'd been in all the previous news coverage, they felt it made more sense to have *me* talk to Oprah. I felt bad about this, even though it wasn't my choice — why couldn't we *both* sit on that sofa with Oprah? It felt like I'd hogged all the limelight.

But Christie being Christie, she forgave me at once, and my make-up applied now, and the show about to start, they took her off to her seat in the front row. She had to be in place for the whole show, of course, because they needed the seats filled from the start. This was a bummer too, because she'd have preferred to stay with us, but, hey, this was TV, and on TV you did as you were told.

And then I realised I needed to use the bathroom.

★   ★   ★

For all the time I spend thinking about George and the bathroom (Does he need to go yet? Should I take him out just in case? If we drive here, will he last out? Does he need to go before bed?), it's amazing that at the pretty mature age of forty-four, I can fail to remember to go myself.

In my defence, I decided it was probably nerves, but, even so, there was no denying that I'd be called in a half-hour and if I didn't go now, it would make for a potentially uncomfortable interview. The only trouble was that the green room was like a ghost town. Now that the show had started taping, everyone had suddenly disappeared; they'd told me they'd come back when it was call-time. It left me with something of a problem. Dare I leave George in the green room? Would he kick-off? Would he start complaining, in his singular booming fashion, about being left by his dad in this strange room all alone?

I figured I'd have to leave him; there was no real alternative. Surely the green room was far enough away from the studios that his bark wouldn't carry right to them? I wasn't entirely convinced about that, but when you gotta go, you gotta go. So I went.

'George,' I said firmly, as I slipped out the door, 'I won't be long, okay? Don't get stressed. I'll be back in just a second.'

The only trouble was that when I returned to the green room I couldn't see him. No big wet nose came to greet me, no doleful look either — no all-too familiar expression that said, 'Dad, how could you *do* that? How could you leave me in this strange room all by myself?' There was no mistaking it — as dogs his size can't hide so easily — George had completely disappeared.

All I could see, when I entered the room a little further, was that the beautiful platter of elegant pastries had been decimated; at least half of them had disappeared along with him. Indeed, as I walked, I felt a squish underfoot. One of them now clung to my shoe.

Panicked, I turned on my heels and went out again. Now I thought about it, as I'd entered the latch hadn't clicked. They had those slow-closing doors and perhaps, when I'd left, the door hadn't been one hundred per cent closed. Either that, or someone else had come in while I was absent, and taken George somewhere. But where? They surely wouldn't have taken him to the studio without me, would they? I checked my watch. Why would they? It wasn't time yet. Of course, the worst-case scenario, and the one that chilled me most, was that George had got out of there all by himself, and was now trotting around loose, God only knew where.

I jogged back up the corridor, choosing to head right, on instinct, and peering into open doorways as I went, without success. I was on about my fourth room when, on exiting, I almost smacked headlong into a security guard who'd just come round the corner.

He was a big guy, this fella, a whole foot taller than I am — and I'm tall — and probably double my weight, though I might exaggerate. He looked at me unsmilingly, like I was completely nuts, but with no time for explanations I decided just to smile and edge past him — it was almost show-time, and I'd mislaid the star, after all.

Happily, or unhappily, depending on what he thought I was up to, he followed, and two doors further down, in another, bigger green room, we eventually caught sight of my disappearing mutt. I was lucky — it was pitch dark, but just before I gave up, I saw a glint of something white out of the corner of my eye.

George was sprawled on a huge sofa, looking all cool and proprietorial. The only thing missing was a serving wench, feeding him grapes.

The security guy and I herded him back into our green room, where he glanced at the remaining pastries, took a long, loving sniff, then looked at me, his expression saying, 'Whatever.'

I thought about scolding him, but decided on a team talk instead. He didn't ask to be left in a room full of pastries, did he? Nor to be left alone with the irresistible prospect of a slightly open door. I was so glad to have him back, I couldn't be cross with him, and we sat and chilled together till the call finally came. We had five minutes: time to wipe the drool from his chops and check my shoes for any clinging smears of pastry.

But George hadn't quite finished stressing me yet. As he got up, the action was accompanied by a familiar and air-rattling sound from his rear, followed, as night follows day in these cases, by the inevitable, nose-wrinkling smell. The pastries, I thought. Great.

As I held my nose and fanned the air, I issued one last instruction. 'Please, George. *Please* don't fart on Oprah.'

22

And The Winner Is . . .

As these things, I'm sure, have a habit of doing, the whole show went by in a blur.

It started, as it turned out, with something of a bang. Or, if not a bang, at least a very loud noise.

The deal was that George and I waited just behind the set, while Oprah did an opening piece about George, and introduced the film we'd shot two days before. That began, because the director had thought it would look neat, with the crew arriving at the house, and an unseen person ringing the front bell. I would open the door, accompanied by George, and the crew would then follow us both inside.

The key thing, of course, was the doorbell. George had always loved the sound of the doorbell being rung — he still does. He's a sociable guy, and the sound of the doorbell means visitors, so it worked on him just like the plank and chicken trick did. He heard the doorbell, and he knew it was fun time. And for George, the best way he can show he's feeling happy about his visitors is to bark — at the top of his lungs.

Cue the bit on the film, right at the top of the segment, when the cameraman rings our front doorbell. And cue George, behind the stage set, invisible to the audience, starting up a bark so incredibly noisy that Christie swears some people near her actually jumped out of their seats, and at least one lady's hand flew, trembling, to her heart.

But that's George. He does love to make an entrance.

After that, it really did feel like it was over in a flash. I met Oprah, we chatted and she gave George his Guinness certificates, even if she did look just a little bit nervous about getting too close — this was the first time she'd ever clapped eyes on him, of course.

★   ★   ★

We went out back after that, while Christie watched the rest of the show. As shows went, it was pretty incredible. As well as the World's Tallest Dog, they had the World's Tallest Teenager and the World's Fastest Violinist, whose playing blew everyone away. They also had on two artists — an amazingly fast and talented portrait painter, and a guy who created masterpieces using an Etch-A-Sketch.

295

There was a birdman, who got his kicks from jumping off cliffs, some Russian acrobats and some tech-savvy singers as well. And at no point, as far as I could tell, anyway, when I watched it later, did any of the chocolate start to melt.

By the time we were deposited back in our limo in the late morning, it felt like it had all been a dream — a pretty incredible dream, as dreams go, but definitely no less surreal.

After the show, though, we had more practical matters to attend to. George had pooped in the morning, so that was one issue sorted, but by now we knew he'd definitely need a pee. And outside, to our mingled delight and concern, it had begun to snow — really heavily. As we set off, we could see that the brown-tinged mounds, which were all that remained of what had fallen several days back, were rapidly becoming white and pristine again, as they were blanketed in showers of fresh snow-flakes. The sidewalks too, previously gritted and cleared and good to walk on, were likewise rapidly turning white.

'We should try and stop somewhere,' I said to Christie. 'We passed a park on the way, didn't we? Maybe we should try that. What d'you think?'

'I think you're right,' she agreed. 'If this

snow gets a lot heavier, I'm thinking we're going to have problems.'

She didn't know it at the time, but Christie's words would be prophetic. Right now though, we asked the driver if he'd mind diverting when he could, so that George could get out and do what he had to do.

In the meantime, having had so little time to talk to her properly since the show, I told Christie about George's last-minute dash for freedom. 'Or, at least,' I said, 'his dash to find a green room with a better-appointed couch. We obviously spoiled him last night letting him have the master. He seems to think only celebrity-style sofas will do. Oh, and perhaps, come to think of it, he may have some toilet issues, after all. He also ate about a dozen of those pastries.'

She winced. 'Oh, dear.'

'*Exactly.*' I fanned a hand in front of my face. 'And I've already had a brush with the result.'

She wrinkled up her nose but then shook her head. 'Too soon.'

'Then it must have been that leftover bit of steak I gave him last night, then. Either that or he's getting a case of traveller's tummy.'

'God,' said Christie, wiping condensation from the car window. 'Look at that, hon — it's coming down in buckets! I can't remember the last time I saw snow like this. Must be ten years, minimum. What a sight!'

She reached to pet George, who was looking out the opposite window. What he made of all the white stuff, who knew? She turned back to me. 'I hope he's going to be able to go okay in this. You really don't like this stuff, do you, Georgie boy?'

'Don't worry,' I reassured her. 'He'll be absolutely fine. If he's got to go, he'll go, won't he? Course he will.'

This turned out to be a fine case of famous last words.

We pulled up a few minutes later at the edge of a big park, and the snow was coming so thick and so fast that we could hardly see the outlines of the trees. And it *felt* every bit as snowy and wintry as it looked. As I opened the door, the cold air literally flew into our faces, and the snow with it — a great swirl of it came in. It felt almost as if someone had stood there with a pail of it and lobbed it right at us just for fun.

Come on, boy,' I said, having clambered out, head down, onto the sidewalk, and pulling encouragingly on George's leash.

It took about two seconds for George, who'd normally be bounding out behind me, to decide that he wasn't going anywhere. In fact, he sat and looked at me as if I was crazy.

I managed to get his front legs out and onto the kerb — having caught him off guard — but after that, well there was no way our dog was going anywhere. I could do what I pleased, but he was definitely not coming. Would I perhaps like to try and make him? Good luck.

Christie stifled a giggle as she sat and watched this tableau. 'You know, hon,' she said, finally, after five fruitless minutes. 'You have to practice what you preach here. He's going *nowhere*.'

She was right. I'd said it so much she was probably sick of hearing it: you can't make two hundred and forty-five pounds of dog do *anything* he doesn't want to do.

I climbed back into the limo and George rearranged himself again, plopping his chin down on his front legs and sighing, then giving me a disgruntled sort of look.

'You're right,' I said, through teeth that wouldn't work right for chattering. 'We'll just have to try again later, I guess.'

'I guess,' said Christie, ducking to avoid a shower as I shook the snow off. 'Fingers crossed, it eases up a bit.'

Some hope . . .

★ ★ ★

In fact, the snow didn't ease up at all, it just got heavier and heavier. So by early evening, with just an hour before we had to leave for the airport, we figured we were waiting for an 'ease up' that simply wasn't going to happen, so we wrapped up as warmly as we could against the bitter cold, and ventured back onto the streets to try again.

They'd shovelled the sidewalks, which was a relief to us both, but unless we let George go on the sidewalk, he'd have to cross huge, growing mounds of new snow to get anywhere suitable to use. And every minute that passed the situation got worse. The snowflakes were coming down hard and fast now, falling in fluffy discs the size of quarters, backlit golden by the street lamps. But while Christie and I were loving the prettiness of the scenery, this was also the last straw of a long and tiring day — George was not happy about being out in this *at all*. He didn't seem to the have the first idea what to make of it. All he knew was that he really didn't like it. This stuff came down, it stuck to him, it made him shiver, it felt icy and, worse, it was all over the ground beneath his paws, too — something he didn't like one little bit.

'Like water, only worse,' laughed Christie, as we watched his reaction. Just as he did when he was a puppy by our pool, he was

300

hopping around, alternately picking up his paws, looking not so much like a dog but a show pony — a show pony doing a spot of dressage, perhaps, or one of those prancing horses you used to see at the circus.

You could tell by his expression that he was seriously Not Amused. And by his demeanour that there was NO WAY he was going to use the bathroom — not now the bathroom had become an outpost of the Arctic. This was a dog who'd been born in Oregon but raised in Arizona, after all.

'We need to find somewhere dry for him,' I told Christie as we walked down the street. We had both put on an extra layer of clothing since earlier, but it still felt like the frosty air was seeping through it.

She stopped and waved a gloved hand around. 'Yeah, but *where*, exactly? Look around you. There must be six inches of snow now, at least!'

'There must be a park somewhere — '

'Which will be covered in snow too — this is Chicago.'

I grinned. 'But I'm guessing they still have dogs here.'

'Who are *used* to snow, honey.'

'But there'll be *somewhere*.'

That somewhere was proving to be pretty elusive. We walked the length of one block, and then we walked another, with George getting more and more cross as we did so. We walked so far that I wasn't altogether sure where we were now, but finally we reached a big intersection.

The snow was beginning to settle on the roads now, and George, we could tell, was becoming desperate. He was getting real antsy, sniffing everything, looking all around him, shuffling his paws so his front and back legs were close together. He needed the bathroom pretty badly. 'Let's go this way,' Christie suggested. 'Maybe there's a — '

'No, wait!' I pointed. 'How about that building over there?'

'Where? Which one?' She followed the direction of my outstretched finger, one hand clamped tightly around the scarf at her neck. With the wind whipping round the corner, it felt fiendishly cold now. The tip of her nose, I noticed, had grown pink. 'That place?' she asked. We both peered to make out the building in the darkness, our vision obscured by the thickly falling flakes.

I nodded. 'It's some sort of community hall, isn't it? Or, wait. Is it a church?'

I looked up, blinking the snow from my eyes. There was a neon-lit white crucifix high on the wall of it, and, more importantly, for our purposes, it seemed to have an area out in front of the building that, strangely, the snow hadn't settled on. We started across the junction, which was empty of cars anyway, and as we got closer you could see the church had some sort of forecourt, an area of which was raised up, and looked like it might have been a garden. Only it wasn't, of course. This was Chicago in February. It would be a few months yet before anything would be growing there. The building was mostly dark; there was just one light burning inside, coming from a big window set pretty high in the wall.

'How weird,' commented Christie, as we reached the other sidewalk. 'All this snow around us, and none on there at all.'

It *was* weird. The area was uncovered, so it made no sense. And what was it doing here anyway? It was a small rectangular area, raised about six inches above the forecourt, and it seemed to have no obvious purpose. 'That's wood chipping covering it, isn't it?' said Christie, as we approached it.

I nodded. 'Looks like it. And maybe that's it. Maybe it's warm — you know, like mulch around a plant keeps the heat in. Maybe that's why the snow isn't sticking to it.'

'What d'you think it is? Some sort of remembrance garden, or something?' We both paused then, to contemplate the potential impropriety of having George use a remembrance garden for a bathroom. Hmm. 'Oh — I know!' said Christie suddenly. 'Maybe it's left over from the holidays. Maybe they had a crib and stuff set up here — a nativity scene. I'll bet that's it. I'll bet that's what it is — hey!'

The 'hey!' was because George had yanked violently on the end of the leash. He had no time to join in debates about religion right now.

It didn't matter whether it was a nativity, a garden or a gift sent from heaven. To George it was just a bathroom, and, boy, did he need the bathroom. He was already beginning to squat before Christie had stumbled behind him up the steps, relief written right across his face.

'D'you think it's okay for him to — ' Christie had just begun to say, when behind us we heard a sudden, and very loud, banging. We both jumped. And then swivelled round. There was a shadowy face in the high window, and silhouetted in front of him was the unmistakable vision of an arm, and a fist, rapping furiously on the glass.

'Hey!' we heard him yelling at us. 'Hey, you out there!'

Christie and I exchanged glances. The temptation to make a run for it was powerful.

Even at this distance, he looked seriously pissed off, and he sounded it, for sure. He'd also left the window now, so presumably he was coming out. But George, who was still peeing, was in no position, for the moment, to go anywhere.

Next thing, and it seemed he'd hardly have had the time to get down to us, we could hear the distinctive sound of a bunch of bolts being drawn back from behind the church's heavy wooden doors.

'Hey!' we could hear him yell again, even before the doors opened. And something else, possibly something unrepeatable.

'Obviously not a man of the cloth, then,' said Christie. 'C'mon, honey!' she added, giving a firm tug to George's leash.

At that moment, one of the huge church doors opened with a creak, and a man — a very cross one, the caretaker I imagined — was silhouetted, gesticulating, in the entrance.

'Hey!' he said again, pointing in our general direction. 'You people letting that mutt go the bathroom on my ground!'

He emerged from the doorway, looking murderous and big, just as George had finished and stood up again. The man was approaching now, both arms waving furiously. It was very dark; there was no moon, so he couldn't really see. And because George, like many large dogs, always squatted to pee, it was obvious that he thought we had allowed George on his 'ground' to leave the church a slightly bigger offering. But looking at him, it felt like there was little point in standing around in the freezing cold debating the issue. Besides, George was done, and no harm had been done either.

'Come on,' I said to Christie. 'Let's go!'

We headed off at a jog, the three of us, back down the snowy sidewalk. George, either traumatised, or thrilled by this unexpected bit of exercise (we thought the latter), had clearly forgotten he didn't like all the white stuff underfoot, and was bounding along beside us, tail thumping happily, ears flapping. I glanced back as we approached the corner. The man was running after us.

'What the *hell?!*' I panted to Christie. 'This guy's seriously pissed at us!'

We ran on, for another fifty yards or so along the sidewalk, stopping only when we reached another intersection, a block along, to catch our breath and see if we'd outgunned him. By now, Christie was laughing so much she was running out of breath, and a little steam had begun to rise from Georgie's flanks. But now his bladder was empty, he seemed to be enjoying himself immensely. His barking — presumably one of pure euphoria — boomed out like cannons in the heavy silence.

I turned around, by now prepared to try and reason with the man, to point out that our 'mutt' had not gone to the bathroom on his 'ground', merely peed, which (I was rehearsing my speech as I thought this) I really didn't think God would strike him down for. But the man had stopped. He'd stopped a good forty feet back, and was just standing, and you could see he was squinting a little — squeezing his eyes up to try and make out exactly what he was seeing through the snow.

'He's just realised,' said Christie, her words making little white clouds in front of her. 'We're standing under this streetlamp, aren't we?' she panted. 'So he can see us. And I think he's only just seen George properly. You know — for the first time. It was pretty dark by that church, wasn't it? That's why he's stopped. I'll bet that's why he's stopped.'

He couldn't have heard her but, as she spoke, we watched the man take a couple of steps backwards, then turn on his heels and jog back towards the church. His parting gesture was nothing more threatening than a scowl.

Christie and I laughed, though not so loudly that he'd hear us and get cross again.

307

He'd clearly decided that some owners, or, rather, some dogs — very big ones — possibly weren't worth having a big blow-out row with. Georgie, unimpressed, snorted out some air and once again started hopping: he'd remembered that he didn't like this snow one little bit.

'I think you're right, hon,' I said to Christie. 'I think you're actually right. How neat is that?' I rubbed my gloved hand over George's head and back. 'How neat is that, Georg-eee, being the world's tallest dog?'

'The world's tallest dog, *ever*. Don't forget that bit,' said Christie. She slipped her hand in mine and we turned to head back. 'The world's tallest dog, ever, who's been on Oprah Winfrey's 'That's Incredible!'.'

'The world's tallest dog, ever, who's been on Oprah Winfrey's 'That's Incredible!', and who spent last night in the master bed in the best suite in the whole of the Omni Hotel.'

'The best suite in the whole of *Chicago*,' added Christie. 'Because he's a celebrated superstar now.' George huffed. 'With the most in-demand paw-tographs on eBay — just you wait. Hey,' she said, snuggling in a little closer. I let go of her hand and put my arm around her instead. 'You think Annabel's giving your mom and pop all kinds of grief?'

'I don't doubt it,' I answered. 'Isn't that

kind of in the job description?' Christie's nose was now bright red. It was very chilly. She looked beautiful, I thought — really beautiful. 'We'll call them up,' I added, squeezing her shoulder firmly, remembering, as if either of us needed to be reminded, that this was the first time we'd ever been parted overnight from our little girl. 'We'll call them just as soon as we're back at the hotel,' I said. 'To see how she's doing, and tell them we'll be home real soon — and all about our trip. What an amazing day! What d'you say, Giant Georgeee? What a day, eh?'

George had no answer, because George couldn't talk, which was probably a plus, because one thing was for sure: George had developed a bit of a taste for superstardom, and we didn't want him getting too full of himself. We didn't want him changing. *Hell*, no.

After all, and it had never seemed so clear to me as that night, he might be an entry in *Guinness World Records*, have a fan club, a website, a whole bunch of followers around the world; he might be unique, and a record-breaker and very, very famous; but the only thing that mattered was that he was part of our family — always had been, always would be. That was *really* what he was.

It was a good feeling for me too, being a

Epilogue

Since being crowned the Guinness World Records' Tallest Living Dog, and Tallest Dog Ever, George has had a real taste of what it's like to be globally famous. On the day of our appearance on *The Oprah Winfrey Show*, all the international news wires were on fire. Word spread very quickly about the new record holder, and news agencies from around the world were hot to get a piece of him.

We were flooded with calls and emails over the next couple of days; it seemed just about everybody wanted to know about George now, and the requests for interviews and appearances kept on piling up. Sleep, for those few days, became a bit of a luxury, as Team Giant George — me, Paul and Dana — struggled to keep up with the sheer volume of communication and make sure no query or request was left unanswered.

And the requests kept right on coming. All the big network news shows wanted to feature Giant George, and all the entertainment shows wanted him too — many of them dispatching crews to come to Tucson to meet us right away. It didn't stop at the Atlantic or Pacific either: TV stations from all over the world wanted to meet George, but flying him internationally was out of the question, so they flew their people in to Tucson instead. In those early weeks I think we entertained television and news crews from some half a dozen different countries around the planet, including Japan, Brazil and Korea, as well as Germany, Spain and Singapore.

But for all the excitement of George's new-found media celebrity, and the thrill of seeing him on film, in news coverage and in print, it was the incredible fans that amazed us the most, and who continue to blow us away today. There's no getting away from it, dog lovers really are a great bunch of people. It doesn't matter where in the world they live — and Giant George fans seem to live almost everywhere — they are one great big worldwide community. George's first You-Tube video has had over 1 million hits by the end of 2010; by any yardstick, that's an awful lot of viewers. He also has over 75,000 fans on Facebook, 2,500 on Twitter, and the traffic on his website — incredibly — is still growing; he now sees around 5,000 visitors a day.

And these people don't just visit to say hi to George, either. They talk to each other too;

they share their stories and anecdotes, post pictures, swap tips and tell their fellow fans about their own beloved pets. They also respond to all the updates we try to post daily — it's a big job for the team to keep up with them all!

★ ★ ★

But George, being a superstar, doesn't have to worry about logistics. Why should he? Heck, he has staff to do all that stuff, doesn't he? It sure feels like it. We're all of us agreed on one thing: we have no time, these days, for any other kind of hobby. Just keeping up with everything we need to keep up with — from running the media to shipping merchandise, to dealing with paperwork, to answering the thousands of emails — occupies more 'happy hours' than we ever imagined.

I'm still busy remodelling houses and have finally finished work on ours now. Christie works way too hard, looking after her many clients, and still manages to be the best mom a little girl could ever wish for. Our little girl, incidentally, is doing great, which doesn't mean she's different from any other toddler — she tests George's patience on a daily basis. Not surprisingly, since she's such an adventurous young lady, she sees him as one giant climbing mountain — one she's determined to conquer. If anyone's gonna saddle him, Annabel will. And we have more excitement lined up on the home front. As I write this, Christie is pregnant! We are expecting a baby boy in May of 2011, arriving a couple of months before *Giant George* the book is published.

As for George himself, well, a typical day goes something like this: get up, have the staff attend to his *toilette* and pedicure, breakfast on the patio, sign a few pawtographs, wait for the limo to take him off somewhere swanky for lunch with friends . . .

No, of *course* it doesn't. Our Georgie is a *dog*! So he tends to spend his days doing what dogs like doing best: he eats, plays and sleeps (oh, and he still does those poops!), and that's pretty much all he *wants* to do.

Of course, he still enjoys plenty of public appearances too. Now we've started figuring out ways he can use his fame to give something back to the community, he's busy with a pretty packed programme. He visits all sorts of places, from schools and play centres to nursing homes — anywhere where being himself is all that's required. Oh, and he's even strutted his stuff on the catwalk, with his mom, for a big charity fashion show fundraiser. Naturally, being George, he loves every single moment, especially when he gets to have his photograph taken, and even more when he gets to have his ears scratched.

But *Oprah* wasn't the last time George flew across America. In September 2010, we got another call from Guinness, and a question: would the World's Tallest Dog like to meet the World's Smallest Dog? They were about to launch the 2011 version of their iconic records book, and wanted these two to provide the 'face' of the launch.

The World's Smallest Dog — Boo Boo — is a real doggie diva. She's a diminutive four-inch-high long-haired Chihuahua, and she was crowned back in 2007. She's also a real pro, another star performer, and we knew she and George would get along famously. Once again, we were off on a high-altitude adventure — only this time we went to New York! And, happily, this time, it being fall, it wasn't snowing. We had an incredible trip — George found the whole thing a blast — and you can find out all about it on his website.

★   ★   ★

So all in all, it's a dog's life, and we're so lucky to share it. Not with the 'Tallest Dog in the World Ever' — though that's great — but

315

with our Georgie, who, first and last, is our much cherished pet. And we're lucky too, that one of the calls that came in after Guinness was from a publisher — *this* publisher — who had a great idea. Would we like to tell the world a little more about our amazing dog?

Hell, yes! So here it is. Thanks for reading.

Dave and Christie x

If you want to know more about what Giant George is currently up to, you can find him in the following places:

www.giantgeorge.com
www.facebook.com/giantgeorge
www.twitter.com/giantgeorgeaz

We do hope that you have enjoyed reading this large print book.

Did you know that all of our titles are available for purchase?

We publish a wide range of high quality large print books including:
Romances, Mysteries, Classics
General Fiction
Non Fiction and Westerns

Special interest titles available in large print are:
The Little Oxford Dictionary
Music Book
Song Book
Hymn Book
Service Book

Also available from us courtesy of Oxford University Press:
Young Readers' Dictionary
(large print edition)
Young Readers' Thesaurus
(large print edition)

For further information or a free brochure, please contact us at:
Ulverscroft Large Print Books Ltd.,
The Green, Bradgate Road, Anstey,
Leicester, LE7 7FU, England.
Tel: (00 44) **0116 236 4325**
Fax: (00 44) **0116 234 0205**

Other titles published by
The House of Ulverscroft:

GENTLE JOHNNY RAMENSKY

Robert Jeffrey

Johnny Ramensky was notorious for being the foremost safe blower of his era. His tough upbringing in the Gorbals was followed by a life of crime and years in jail, but his expertise in explosives gave him a chance to serve his country. When the Second World War broke out, Ramensky joined the elite Commandos. Time after time he would show exceptional bravery as he was parachuted behind enemy lines. He would blow open the safes of the German High Command to secure documents vital to the war effort. Ramensky was an extraordinary man, criminal and war hero, who wore the Green Beret with pride.

HOPE STREET

Pamela Young

Pamela Young's family lived in the heart of Horwich, near Manchester, in Hope Street. Her family had a unique gift passed down from generation to generation: the women of the family were able to communicate with the Spirit worlds. Pamela's memories are of her mother's Spiritualist friends arriving for one of her sittings. She describes how, after her mother's death, she was in the depths of despair, but found her own spiritual gift. And guided by the spirit of her mother, she finally understood the prophecy and message of hope for humanity that Spirit had been working to bring to the world.

A SEAL PUP IN MY BATH

Steve Greenhalgh

Having worked as an RSPCA inspector since the early 1970s, Steve Greenhalgh has been involved in some rare adventures . . . Few people have joined a police raid on a quail-fighting ring, or gassed themselves with chloroform while driving a van. He's wrestled swans in high street traffic. And on a fast-flowing river, with one oar, he paddled a boat to save a cat, while Rolf Harris provided a running commentary for *Animal Hospital*. Some of Steve's experiences are of a more serious nature, but they illustrate the vital work done by the RSPCA and its impact on ordinary people's lives.